A SEASON IN THE DESERT

a season in the desert

MAKING TIME HOLY

W. PAUL JONES

PARACLETE PRESS
BREWSTER, MASSACHUSETTS

Library of Congress Cataloging-in-Publication Data

Jones, W. Paul (William Paul)
    A season in the desert : making time holy / W. Paul Jones.
        p. cm.
    Includes bibliographical references.
        ISBN 1-55725-249-1
        1. Spiritual life—Catholic Church. 2. Space and time—
    Religious aspects—Catholic Church. I. Title.
    BX2350.65 .J66 2000
    263—dc21   00-009818

10 9 8 7 6 5 4 3 2 1

© 2000 by W. Paul Jones
ISBN 1-55725-249-1

Published by Paraclete Press
Brewster, Massachusetts
www.paracletepress.com

Printed in the United States of America.

Dedicated to
The Hermitage Spiritual Retreat Center—
an ecumenical dream
where sacred time and space
surround searchers with depth,
and the driven are cloaked with peace.

Season: "the action of sowing; a time or period made significant by a particular feature, circumstance, or event; something that gives relish, taste, or flavor."

+ + + + +

"Let there be lights in the dome of the sky to separate the day from the night; and let them be for signs and for seasons and for days and years."
(GEN. 1:14)

"God . . . knows your going through this great desert."
(DEUT. 2:7)

"The wilderness and the dry land shall be glad, the desert shall rejoice and blossom . . . with joy and singing."
(ISA. 35:1–2)

"For everything there is a season, and a time for every matter under heaven:
a time to be born, and a time to die;
a time to plant, and a time to pluck up what is planted;
a time to kill, and a time to heal;
a time to break down, and a time to build up;
a time to weep, and a time to laugh;
a time to mourn, and a time to dance;
a time to throw away stones, and a time
to gather stones together;
a time to embrace, and a time to refrain from embracing;
a time to seek, and a time to lose;
a time to keep, and a time to throw away;
a time to tear, and a time to sew;
a time to keep silence, and a time to speak;
a time to love, and a time to hate;
a time for war, and a time for peace."
(ECCLES. 3:1–8)

"[God] has made everything suitable for its time;
moreover [God] has put a sense of past and
future into [our] minds."
(ECCLES. 3:11)

"When the fullness of time had come, God sent his Son."
(GAL. 4:4)

"I will bless the Lord at all times."
(PS. 34:1)

Too late am I alone to think
that I am ready now to start.
What years ago I once began
not know 'til ending time
I hunch where best to start.
I know it now not what I know,
but what I know to search —
and sigh at life once set upon
an always moving on.
Once all depended on east or west
Or up and down.
But once my moving began to stop,
'twas then it was
my start began.

—W. *Paul Jones*

CONTENTS

Chapter Four:

A SEASON IN THE DESERT

CHAPTER ONE

An Overture

Looking Back

I remember vividly one particular evening conversation with my Abbot. I shared the deep loneliness I was experiencing. It had nothing to do with friends, for I have many. It was a deeper loneliness, way down where life seems to issue forth. As we talked, the thought began to emerge that I am a "bridge person." The more I shared my pilgrimage, the more I could see the image of one of those old medieval bridges with shops and residences built onto the bridge itself. It wasn't that this bridge which was me did not function in crossing from one shore to the other. But the difficulty was more that of living *on* the bridge so that I could hold together within myself the polarities of both shores, sides that seemed resistant, at times even hostile, to being held together.

My life as *bridge* seemed to begin at least as far back as my birth. Although I was not told until later, I somehow knew that my "emergence" was a life-and-death struggle with my mother. In the hospital waiting room, my father had been told that I would die in the process, but his wife would probably make it. Within half an hour, the nurse's report was the opposite. Finally, she returned with the news that while both of us would make it, we were both exhausted by the ordeal. So it would be for years to come, in a bridging of death and life. To this day I have a mark on each side of my head from being forcefully wrenched out in order to live.

I am coming to realize, however, that the ensuing life-long struggle between my mother and me may be a parable for the pilgrimage of all of us. Scripture calls it a visiting of the sins (or needs) of the parents on the children, at least unto the third and fourth generation. It was not until later in life that I finally saw how much my intense "doing" was an effort to earn from my mother the words, "Paul, I love you." They never came. They couldn't, for she never could "wrench forth" from her father those same words that she also craved. And I stood in the middle between the two of them: an only child, as the one who, in doing everything "right," might be her claim to him of being a deserving mother. Although I was never a successful bridge between them, my drive to try was to guarantee that I had sufficient value not to be thrown away. On the bridge, I directed traffic.

Appalachia was the "home" of my childhood, in a tiny western Pennsylvania coal-mining town, with the houses propped up against the side of a hill. My father was born down by the sulfur creek, a swamp they called Frog Hollow, located on the "wrong side" of the tracks. His schooling ended in the third grade, after which his job was to lead the mules in and out of the mines, pulling the loaded "dinky cars." My remembrance of the mines is lying flat on my back, twenty-two miles into the mountain, listening oh-so-carefully after a cave-in as the earth creaked; I was responsible for deciding if the vein was safe enough for the miners to crawl in and dig. One never loses this sense of the fragility of life. I saw it in the look of my parents as they embraced each morning, then my father's waving back as he walked down the road to the mine. We were never certain if he would come back alive. He was walking the bridge.

I knew of only two ways out of Appalachia. Moving was never a possibility, for one didn't know what was out there beyond the valley. One legitimate way out was football, but I was far too slender. The other was an academic scholarship. This was my ticket. I started college in a formerly boarded-up grade school in the next town. Since I did not know anyone educated beyond high school, I suspected that "college" even at its worst had to be better than dirt and exhaustion. In time, listening to Beethoven string quartets helps one lose a taste for blue-collar radio music. And there comes a point when manicured lawns can make junk cars on concrete blocks seem a bit unsightly. But one never coughs up all the coal dust. One never forgets, but neither can one ever really go home again. One looks back from the bridge.

I remember sitting on the deck of my new home with my father, having made him proud—for now I was a Yale graduate and a Princeton professor. Looking out toward the golf course, he asked with pride, "How does all this make you feel?" Without a thought, the sound that emerged from my lips was "Pfff." He never understood. But what do you do next when you have a spacious split-level house, two cars, 2.3 fine children, and a collie? More and more was becoming less and less. And where I was sitting, "to have" was slowly "to have not."

Not much later, I was commissioned to do a lecture at a national gathering—and given the nicely defined topic of "God"! Without flinching, I took on the assignment, wrote the lecture, mounted the stage, and accepted with beaming face the standing ovation. Yet somewhere over Nevada, I realized that I was a "functional atheist." Never once had I asked this "God" for help in doing such an impossible task. Nor did I even mutter appreciation to this "God" when the applause came. "I did it myself, thank you!" It made little difference in my living if I believed in a God or didn't. Atheist or believer, as both I found myself sitting lonely on the bridge. And I heard the words in my soul: "Because you are lukewarm, and neither cold nor hot, I am about to spit you out of my mouth" (Rev. 3:16).

This was around the time that my favorite cousin had a severe heart attack. When I visited him in intensive care, I asked the innocuous, commonplace question: "How are you?" The answer was not commonplace. "Terrible! Do you know what it's like just to lie here and have nothing to do but really look at one's life for the first time? If I keep working at it, in fifteen years I'll be given a gold watch and some polite applause, commending me for spending my whole life trying to get people to smoke Camels rather than Lucky Strikes. It sucks. And you only get to go around once."

My own spiritual heart attack was a birthday—my fiftieth. With it came the resolve to take a sabbatical. But instead of going to the Harvard library to write a book on "prayer," thereby not having to do any of it, I took a gamble. I would go to a Trappist monastery where the monks' only reason for being is to pray. They peel carrots to the glory of God. They even wash dishes, I was told, to

6

the same glory. Either I would discover for myself what they knew, or have the courage to disavow the theology that I was spending a lifetime teaching. What I found there may not have been God, at least not directly. But what found me was a yearning, a thirsting, for which the name "God" would have to do. Especially during certain midnight hours, it felt like being damned with the insatiable. Sitting on the bridge, being neither fish nor fowl, the only proof of God I found was that nothing else could any longer satisfy. The ache was the gift of the hidden Presence. On the bridge, I was fishing.

Since then I have become pretty much a misfit on either shore, for I have lost my taste for the "American dream." The three P's—possessions, prestige, and power—these are the rewards promised boldly in each magazine ad. But I was no longer hooked. In fact, I had come to know that they are not really rewards at all, but temptations to soul-selling. Even for Jesus they were the primal temptations: He rejected them not only in the wilderness, but had to continue to reject them, as they tempted him for the rest of his life. "The devil . . . departed from him *until an opportune time*" (Luke 4:13; emphasis added). To struggle between the same reality—as both lure and sin—is to be on the bridge.

The monastery that had touched me kept drawing me back, over and over again. One morning before sunrise, I read in the silence one sentence by the Trappist monk Thomas Merton. He once said, "The beginning of spirituality is to do nothing and feel no guilt!" In a flash I understood deeply about my mother and me. To stop "doing," if only for a day off, was to risk not "being." I remembered vividly her last words to me in a letter she

7

wrote just before her death through self-starvation: "How did we go so wrong with you?" At first I was deeply hurt, once again. Then I knew what she meant. I had thrown away the American dream that had come my way, and had chosen instead to live with the "rejects" who were unacceptable on either end of the bridge: gays, African Americans, prisoners, druggies. To her, in moving to the inner city, I had thrown it all away, and "what would the suburban neighbors think now?" Unconditional Love—nothing less than sheer gift—that alone would be able to heal me. Grace on the bridge.

Strange it was in the months to come, that a Trappist monastery would be the setting in which I experienced for the first time the true meaning of Methodism, the church of my upbringing. I remember as a boy in church-membership class reading a booklet about early Methodism. I was fascinated. "Why don't we do any of this in *our* church?" I asked the pastor. The response was a scowl. Years later I was discovering this heritage, largely abandoned, as the way of life in monasticism, a movement that spans the whole of the Church's history and life. I had taken a vow at my Methodist ordination: "to go on to perfection." Here in the monastery Latin was used to express a similar aim: *conversatio morum,* or the "conversion of life." The two phrases express essentially the same vow—a lifelong transformation of lifestyle.

On either the Catholic or the Methodist shore, such change was seen as possible only through spiritual direction, which supplies a means of supportive accountability. It means living under discipline and being rooted in the daily Eucharist, which Wesley himself insisted upon for his preachers. Whether through the scheduled prayers of

Wesley's "holy club," or the "Daily Office" structuring the monk's day, this was how each life was to be rehearsed in promise.

A Catholic heart was wooing my Protestant mind. But so it was with Wesley. Seeking spiritual renewal within a high-church Anglican context provided the architecture for Wesley's own bridge. When in due time God added to my Methodist ordination of forty years my ordination as a Roman Catholic priest, I was not surprised, for my home on the bridge now had a roof.

But the changes did not stop coming. Wesley's movement began when several persons came to his door, asking for "help in fleeing from the wrath to come." The motive underlying this plea has its contemporary equivalents— as, for example, in the promise that "the family that prays together stays together." In both cases, the motive is self-serving: a "doing" in order to "get." Whereas this might be a spiritual starting place, such motivation is little different from that of the secular world. Only the arena of "gain" is different.

My real *conversatio* emerged one night, as the moon-shadows played gently and mysteriously across my bedspread. In that moment, I knew what experiences were central in order for life to have meaning. They were not for sale, nor were they earned. Expressive of such experiences is one's gasp when one is mesmerized by a vee of geese on their way north, and experiencing the ache Judy Garland knew as she sang, "Birds fly over the rainbow, why then, oh why, can't I?" It is what one "knows" in the intoxication of observing the ocean beating against worn cliffs. One either hears it in Mozart's "Requiem" or one is soul-deaf.

What good are any of these experiences? No good—no good whatsoever. They are in no way useful or productive. Their value is utterly different. It is not instrumental, as in being helpful in acquiring something else. Their value is *intrinsic*—good for their own sake. If one makes love with one's spouse and then rolls over with the words, "What good was that?" Divorce is only a matter of time. Holy uselessness, sabbatical worthlessness, divine leisure—these form the heartbeat of spirituality. To be passionately in love with God's creation, and to "make love" with God, is to lose one's self in ecstasy for its own sake.

In those early days in Appalachia, I saw miners beaten for insisting on a living wage. I was arrested during the civil rights demonstrations of the 1960s. I was a chaplain to the local Black Panther Party. I have consecrated the lifelong commitment of gay couples. I live now as a hermit among the poor, and on a regular schedule I return to the monastery to practice its "socialism" where all things are held in common. I suffer the last day with those on death row who will be executed at midnight. If life is no big deal, then nothing is. But to fall in love with Life and its Source is to live on the bridge—for one inevitably becomes the enemy of everyone and everything that deprives life in its fullness to anyone on either shore. So I live on the bridge between poor and rich, weak and powerful, nonviolent and violent, unemployed and employed, old and young. It is all of a piece.

The shadows deepened that evening in my Abbot's quarters. We lit a candle together. Somehow we both knew then. Somewhere along the line we had both begun living the "bridge life." And together we recognized it as a joyous homelessness. But that was not all. Before we embraced for the evening, we dared to believe that it wasn't just two pilgrimages that had come within hailing distance of one another. We dared to believe that ours were variations on the plot claiming all of us who are called Christians. Back in my cell, the night reading suggested the final bridge. As "strangers and foreigners on the earth," we are "seeking a homeland," "a better country," a "heavenly one" (Heb. 11:13–16).

Looking Ahead

I remember developing what I called "exposure experiences" as part of my teaching methods, so that students would walk the mean streets of the inner city, or touch death by conducting a funeral at the morgue for a nameless body fished from the Missouri River. Although I resisted at first, I came to see the wisdom in the students' insistence upon some guide by which to "recognize what it is that we are supposed to see." So let me do the same for the reader. We can walk with a quick gait through the heart of the chapters to follow.

CHAPTER TWO Before we were born, each of us was embraced by the warm oceanlike sounds of the moving maternal liquid in which we were being formed. Each of us was soothed or enlivened by the wind-sounds echoing through the chambers of our mother's lungs. And with the first flutterings of our own hearts, we learned the music of counterpoint in relation to the varying rhythms of the maternal heartbeat.

Anxiety, joy, fear, ecstasy, worry, restlessness—all are moods characterizing the kaleidoscope of our mother's pilgrimage that affected profoundly the tempo and texture of the space-time world of our own formation before birth. And when the time for exit came, for some it was like an escape. For others, it was more like an exile. Whichever way, whether we crave a return to the Eden-like womb, or a frantic thrust for a "kingdom" yet to be—for all of us life is, inevitably, a *pilgrimage*. It is *the dream of return, versus the tragic, creative call forward*. Deep within our souls is the memory of this initial formation. Little wonder it is that youth identify so readily with the relentless beat of acid rock, for it recalls the beat of the maternal chamber. Elders can sit for hours by restless surf, for even aging cannot erase the liquid surging of one's prenatal home. Understandably as well, something deep within us responds to movement: to wind in one's hair, or to the sight of a soaring bird, or the longing we feel when we stand alone at the end of a tugging kite string. In sounds, too, we were conceived. So we find comfort even in the sounds of an unattended radio in the next room, or we switch on a TV we have no intention of watching. These are the makings of liturgies and sacraments that clothe our naked souls.

Hard though life is, our foraging is really for the little meanings. Traditionally, boys can settle for a frog and dirt. Girls can make a doll out of anything, rocking to sleep a handkerchief-wrapped clothespin. Our needs later may take the shape of a house of one's own, or a place where one truly belongs, or a simple task enfolded within a sense of something larger. But all of these are tokens and souvenirs of the craving for "home"—even though it is actually for a place we have never been before. And the strength to persevere is rooted in hearing, occasionally along the journey, the three simple words of love. Novels have chapters; dramas have acts; music has movements, and life . . . ? Blessed are those who recognize their parts, believe in the invisible playwright, and dance to the silent conductor. Henri Nouwen was right when he wrote that one can best detect the meaning of time in the emptiness of the desert.

CHAPTER THREE So, too, the time of the cosmos is shaped by pilgrimage. The opening passage of the Bible conjures the image of Spirit moving over the face of mystery which is void and without form (Gen. 1:2). And history as the big picture is acted and reenacted within each creature, as the spirit within echoes the Spirit without and moves over the unconscious void, inspiring it to take form. Self-consciousness is this ability of the Spirit to recognize one's spirit, greeting itself in a birth of freedom, compassion, memory, and anticipation.

But this pilgrimage outward can be aborted and turn in upon itself. It then can manifest itself as fear of the unknown, or an environment that strangles one in loneliness, or an emptiness which, lacking promise, can only be stuffed into submission. Whatever the path, consciousness is both terrifying and exhilarating, often causing one to crouch in the shadowed corners of the unconscious. True "going home" begins when one's spirit recognizes the Spirit within as one's grounding companion, and the Spirit without is discerned to be the lure of the cosmos from formless void into history and the call to ongoing creativity.

This pilgrimage of spirit with Spirit is what we mean by "spirituality." It is most identifiable in the rhythm forming the plot of one's autobiography. Since no one, then, is implicitly devoid of spirituality, a primal task is to render one's spirituality self-conscious. By being discerned into speech, "spirituality" is birthed into "theology."

CHAPTER FOUR "Theologizing" is the name for this task of rendering spirituality as pilgrimage into self-consciousness. So it is with the Church, in which this task results in "doctrines" by which the Church stores the heritage of its own pilgrimage. Taken alone, these doctrines are meaningless, for as attempted answers to the universal questions raised by each person's pilgrimage, they make no sense without the questions. Thus one of our tasks is to articulate these questions for which the key doctrines of Christianity are meant to be lived as answers. Rituals, in turn, are the emotion-laden stations along the way for rehearsing both question and answer—within a landscape otherwise quite bleak.

CHAPTER FIVE For many persons, time is one-dimensional, experienced as one damn thing after another. In contrast, the gift of the Church is to open up the richness of time's multidimensionality, where time can be lived in its fullness. To question time's holistic meaning is first to explore *cosmic time*—the spectacular drama of expansiveness, so inconceivable as to need the abstraction of "light years," billions of them. Then *eternal time* emerges in the context of our particular world, visible through Scripture itself as the pilgrimage from Eden to the Kingdom, from the creation to consummation. *Cultural time* focuses on the power of symbol—giving birth and bringing death to the meaning inherent in each society. Here one recognizes the ongoing rhythms of "dark ages" and "renaissances."

Historical time, in the sense we will use it, refers to the distinctive pilgrimages of both groups and individuals that result in separate, alternative "worlds." My research identifies five such "theological worlds," out of which can spring, when it is not recognized, the pain and violence of competitiveness, rivalry, and hostility within both secular realms and the pluralism of the Church. *Life-time* points to the particular plot that gives shape to one's autobiography, which one is called both to recognize and to forge. *Sabbath* or *Jubilee time* is a special time grounded in God's "seventh day" of rest after creating and reenacted as Israel's year of agricultural restoration every seventh year. It is echoed in the call for economic redistribution to be observed at the end of the seventh period of seven years. Whatever its length, without periodic sabbatical or *Jubilee* observances, time becomes relentlessly destructive.

CHAPTER SIX   In the sixth chapter, we move beyond the various ways in which, for the Christian, time is *structured* to the diverse ways in which time is *lived*. *Yearly time* has been claimed and powerfully shaped by the Church over the years, to be experienced as liturgical seasons. These are lived as the rhythms of anticipation and fulfillment, fasting and feasting, repentance and celebration. While most time in the Western world is solar based, *monthly time* allows for a lunar impact on our biological rhythms. *Weekly time* is the division of life's flow based on the Church's recognition of Sundays as "little Easters," placing the distractions and dilemmas of our work-a-day week in proper perspective. *Daily time* has been distilled best within the monastic tradition. Here the Church has forged what it means to live as Jesus instructed—"do not be anxious about

15

tomorrow." (Matthew 6:34). And for the final richness of time as lived, we will explore momentary time, ordinary time, and timelessness.

CHAPTER SEVEN The Triduum, the three days from Maundy Thursday to Easter, has been so central to the Church's life in time that we will devote an entire chapter to it. We will describe the events and liturgy of these days in such a way as to experience why the Church has declared the Triduum to be the primal *time event* in which the whole meaning of Christianity is best experienced and understood. With this primary event of time within time, we will end.

The primary significance of Christian spirituality is its power to sacralize time and space. While these two ultimately cannot be separated, this volume will focus primarily on the sacralizing of *time*. Another volume to follow, *A Table in the Desert*, will focus on *space*, exploring in turn how time so wraps "things" that *space* likewise becomes sacred. Together, time and space form the jeweled arena in which Christian spirituality emerges. No matter what *other*-worldly arena may await us, Christianity is the most *this*-worldly religion to have appeared, its meaning wrapped in a spatio-temporal cloak.

CHAPTER TWO

Birth as a Religious Event: Beginning the Spiritual Journey

"It was you who . . . knit me together in my mother's womb. . . .
I am fearfully and wonderfully made." (Ps. 139:13–14)
"I am a pilgrim on the earth." (Ps. 119:19 GRAIL)
"I hear a voice I had not known." (Psalm 81:5)

1. The Prebirth Context

Life is complex. For nine months before what we call "birth," we are already on a pilgrimage. That we cannot pinpoint the exact moment when "life" begins witnesses to the fact that all of life is composed of ongoing events that are increasingly manifold and immensely mysterious. One of the most formative of these events occurs within the womb itself in what can best be identified as a religious or theologizing process.

Surrounded by a warm and embracing fluid, "early life" is formed within a "home" distinctive to a very particular mother. She, in turn, continues to be shaped by characteristics and circumstances that converge as her own unique and ongoing autobiography. Particularly formative in this mutual interacting between mother and child are two experiences. On the one hand are the sounds of the relentless expansion and contraction of the mother's lungs, accompanied by the gurgles and swishing of this watery home. Little wonder that humans have a fascination with the multiple sounds of water in general and the ocean's relentless surf in particular. Herman Melville wisely observed in the beginning of his *Moby Dick* that every human path ends eventually at water.

The second formative feature is the relentless beating of the mother's heart, amplified in the sound chamber of the womb. It is little wonder that the beat of music is so attractive to us. In fact, current research shows that various tempos of music stimulate corresponding responses in the fetus. This impact is particularly true if the mother likes to sing. Every loud "boom box" carried down the street is in fact a simulation through deep memory of prebirth existence. Growing teenagers in particular lose themselves in the demanding and unifying beat of popular music, feeling strangely at home with that which defies every distraction.

Blessed is the "prebirth life" being formed by a mother's steady and mesmerizing heartbeat. The cadence is a "lullaby" of trust, echoing softly and reliably through the chambers of the heart. Blessed, too, is the new life for whom the air chambers emit a tranquil, comforting, and steadfast flow. Together, these two "spiritualizing" sounds define functionally the meaning of "home"—for better or worse. Thus it is that those who are blessed by positive surroundings continue, long after birth, to be touched deeply by the sound of a breeze through willows, water lapping at the shore, a bird's persistent call for the sun to appear. These sounds, and hundreds more, bring us "home," if only for a moment. Understandably, Ernest Bloch throughout his writings defines religion as the yearning for home.

I still remember a day when I was building my hermitage in the quiet, deep softness of a cedar forest. A teenager delivered a truckload of lumber. He hesitantly got down from the truck. "Do you live here?" "Yes." "Kinda spooky, isn't it? . . . What on earth do you do? Any other people around here?" With the delivery quickly completed, he walked even more quickly to his cab. "I sure hope I know how to get out of here." With radio blasting and wheels spinning, he made a rapid exit. I knew what he did not: that what was haunting him was going with him down the dusty road. And, sooner or later, it would eat its way into him until he yearned for a "re-birthing"—until he yearned for "home."

We are destined to work and rework for a lifetime the sounds and feelings of our becoming, whether they were strangely nourishing or relentlessly depriving. These dynamics of formation and deformation and reformation will always be at work, as sunlit warmth and stalking shadows form one's ongoing kaleidoscope, luring and threatening, demanding and freeing, yearning and peaceful. They will always be there, no matter what circumstances evoke them. It is hard to overrate the external factors that are invasive or expansive throughout our first nine fragile months. Branding us is a mother's temper and the anguish that tempers even the feel of her voice. Extended times of anxiety, a flaring of anger, a fear for one's safety—these force the heartbeat to race in uncertainty and the lung's sounds to be rapid and shallow. The womb contorts and shrinks in the invasive emotions of upheaval, or flexes and expands in the expansive emotions of joy.

The kaleidoscope of emotional nuances, the particularity of the maternal lifestyle, just as surely as the biological markings of DNA, imprint the emerging life with the footprints of the parents—unto the third and fourth generation. This helps to account for why adopted children often have difficulty growing steadily, without major trauma.

19

No matter how much the adoptive parents provide a welcoming environment, more times than not a negative "primal image" remains. During the long and deep months of birthing, the formative mother may have been obsessed with the guilt of having been foolish, a fear of being found out, or a sense of being abandoned or betrayed. And all the time, the unfortunate and undesired "growth" in one's womb relentlessly takes claim of her body. This may be accompanied by angry arguments by the birth parents. This contest experienced by the "early life," can be as terrifying as when young children hear from their dark beds the fights in the kitchen.

For this primal prebirth period, the mother's heartbeat is often adrenaline-driven, her breath short and nervous. To the sensitive, fragile, and totally dependent fetus, such sensations convey early and persistently a physical negativity that borders on an unconscious nightmare. When the pregnancy is a mistake, unwanted, or even despised, such an attitude can reduce the "young life" to the status of an invading tumor. What an incredible burden, to be trapped in such a womb, and fiercely unwanted. The internal birthing pilgrimage, then, can become a frantic life-and-death struggle, intersected by perhaps a mother's "prayers" for a miscarriage. The inability of the fetus to be self-sustained renders futile its frantic efforts to escape from its containment, as useless as the woman's own nightmare of being "discovered."

What is equally frightening is how much one word persistently echoes and re-echoes in most of our post-birth pilgrimages—that of being "unwanted" and, thus, "discardable." The feelings of the mother are, strangely, the emerging feelings of the child, although the volume can differ greatly. This makes understandable why many adopted children crave to break the silence surrounding their adoption, demanding of the birthing mother: *"Why?"* New techniques, such as water delivery, may provide a more hospitable debut, and yet rarely do any of us really escape this "adoption syndrome." Are there any of us who are not haunted by the feeling of being unwanted, an intruder, a mistake—an alien? In my many years of doing spiritual direction, I have yet to work with a person who has not thought, sometimes, "If you really knew me, you wouldn't like me!"

Some years ago the freshman class where I was teaching had no sense of unity, apparently composed of competitive "cliques." I was asked to work with them. My first act was to pass out small pieces of paper, with the instructions to write "yes" or "no" in answer to this question: "Do you feel as if you belong to this class?" Not surprisingly, the response was 79 "no," 0 "yes." The issue was not that some of the students were being left out, but that the condition of the class was such that no one felt as if they belonged. As I continued to work with them, it became clear that I was not dealing with a unique class. What was involved was the ever-present *human condition*. Deep inside so many of us are stories of being chosen last in playground games. Once it became clear to this class that no one belonged, a new sense of belonging strangely emerged.

These observations lead to the conclusion *that birth itself is literally a forced exile, and we emerge as an alien in a foreign land.* The child's birthing occurs most often to the sounds of pained cries, heavy breathing, and frightened heartbeat, with the child itself squeezed and often distorted. Gone is the liquid home; indeed it has probably broken.

21

There is the legendary slap by a doctor to the child held upside-down, in order to awaken and force the child to begin the pilgrimage, suddenly, on his or her own. Independent, yet dependent, the new infant searches for a breast that may or may not be available. Crying is the direct response—fundamentally a craving to "go home." For some, the cry parallels that of the Israelites: "Why did you bring us up out of Egypt, to kill us . . . with thirst?" (Exod. 17:3). Here was a conflict between the Israelites' craving to go back to a place that was not "home," versus the courage to escape to a "Promised Land" where they had never been before. So it is with each of us. We live on the bridge.

2. The Craving for Home

The Church, from its inception, has recognized this human condition, calling it "the fall," or what I call "originating sin." It is experienced as a state of existing in fear of leaving a womb that to some degree has been "home." Or it is the ardor to flee from the repulsion of the maternal prison in a pilgrimage that resembles a "desert." For all of us, it is either or both, but never neither. Perhaps "exile" is the most appropriate word for this bewildering and traumatic transition from prebirth to postbirth existence.

No matter how unpredictable, unstable, inconstant, or precarious the prebirth formation, the driving dynamic within each of us, from birth on, is to find "home." I remember distinctly the response of the audience when in homesickness the alien creature uttered the words "E.T., phone home." There was a gasp of identification throughout the audience. My immediate thought was how fortunate E.T. was. Apparently he knew the phone number.

The Old Testament is composed of many kinds of writings and many dissimilar authors. When exiled during the Babylonian Captivity, the Hebrews cried out, "How could we sing the Lord's song in a foreign land?" (Ps. 137:4). In time, the answer became clear: by telling the stories of who they were, and thus who we are. We call "redactors" those editors who collected these writings, endeavoring to make of them an integrated whole. It appears that they felt the need to help the reader understand how all these writings fit together. So they chose an "introduction," functioning much like an "overture" does in Broadway musicals. Then, when heard later, the hearers would recognize the theme. The story they chose was that of Adam and Eve. The redactors recognized in its plot *the* pervading and persistent theme of history itself. Only the names of the characters change: Adam and Eve become Cain and Abel, then Abraham and Lot—all the way to Jesus and Judas.

This primal story functions as a parable, with dual meanings. First, the story of Adam and Eve portrays the beginning of history itself as one of exile. Secondly, it portrays the plight of each individual. With the emergence of self-conscious life, humans become alien to the teeming world of "living things" and are forced to struggle with anxiety and awareness of death. In humans, finitude is somehow at odds with itself.

So deep is this contrast between "self" and "world" that it is not too strong to identify the emergence of *homo sapiens* as the birthing of a freak. Birth sets the parameters of living—for self and for race—as a journey through the

23

desert, yearning for God. But in our anxiety of not belonging, our natural drive for self-preservation becomes premeditated—and sin makes a desert out of all it touches.

3. Death and Anxiety

The "freakiness" that characterizes our existence focuses in one fact. While all things without exception die, humans do not "belong" in that they alone are permeated by the knowledge *that they will die.* Other animals express fear, instinctively "knowing" the danger of exposure to other animals, squealing in fright when cornered or even when vulnerable. Fear has an object—the "who" or "what" or "it" that entails danger to one's existence or well being. Quite different is the deepest trait in humans— that of "anxiety." It takes many forms, but in each case the uneasiness or restlessness has no identifiable "object." Rather it is a *state of being,* one pointed to by such books as Soren Kierkegaard's *Sickness Unto Death* and *Fear and Trembling* or Paul Tillich's *The Courage to Be.*

This state of being human we can call "ontic fragility." Using an analogy, millions of electrical objects and systems operate as if they are self-contained, self-sustaining, and independent. Suddenly the power goes out. Everything stops and is plunged into darkness. The instinctive question emerges: "Where did the light go?" Actually the light didn't go anywhere—it simply has ceased to exist. So it is with human life. Death is simply the state of being no longer— stopped, inoperative—and the body rots. And "life"? Like the extinguished light, it is nothing, nowhere at all. We may have the ability to decide what to do with our life, but life itself? Life is a "given" that one either has or doesn't—and the difference is ultimately not ours to say. Ours is to be anxious—for thou fool, tonight, any night, your life may be required of you (Luke 12:20).

Such anxiety arises not only from a threat concerning the end of life. Death is woven into life's very fabric. It is emptiness in the form of an event. This relates to God's creation of the cosmos *ex nihilo*—from nothing. We can best understand this by using our imagination. Imagine a dog. Look at it—what color, how big, what kind—pet it, and throw it a ball. You can do all these things as long as your imagination holds the dog in being. Now, think of a tree. Oops, where did the dog go? It didn't go anywhere—it simply isn't.

God's creation is analogous to our imagination. Thus, we can understand the Christian insistence that God creates *ex nihilo*—by imagination. God cannot create things that don't need God, any more than a machine can pull out its plug and keep running. Thus God as Creator refers not simply to the beginning, but to every moment in which anything exists. Thus for God to forget anything means that in that very instant, it simply would no longer be. The so-called "ontological argument" about the existence of God is really based on experiencing one's self to be absolutely dependent upon God in each moment, without which one is nothing. The other side of the human "I am" is, of necessity, the divine "I am"—as the "Ground" of our being. Inevitably, then, humans have a sense of "ontic fragility"—we are one missed heartbeat away from oblivion. Time would stop if God suffered a memory lapse. And since space is that which *is* whenever anything exists, when there is nothing, space too is gone. Everything.

While we try, madly at times, to quiet this anxiety that comes simply from existing, a further question cannot be quieted: "Is this Ground hospitable?" As we shall see, this question gives a special nature to time and space for the Christian—for everything that *is* points to that without which it would not *be*. So experienced, everything becomes *gift*.

The Adam and Eve parable, then, characterizes not only the story of the race, but the emergence from the womb of each of us, slung as we are between the passion to be "free from" and the yearning to "return to." Scripture characterizes this state as being driven out of the womb-garden of Eden, which is guarded by a flaming sword that at every turn halts re-entry (Gen. 3:23-24). To exist "east of Eden" is to be haunted by "alien" *time*— haunted in the present by the specter of being determined by the past, prematurely cut off by a relentless future. Thomas Wolfe's two great novels provide the parameters for our pilgrimage—*You Can't Go Home Again* and *Look Homeward Angel*. Yet while this longing has a variety of responses, T.S. Eliot, in *Prelude IV*, illustrates well for the Christian the deeper feeling as "the notion of some Infinitely gentle / Infinitely suffering thing."

For both species and self, then, existence is a life-and-death struggle for "home" in a *present* dangling between the pull of the *past* (death wish) and anxiety over the *future* (life wish). William Kraft describes most of us in these times when he says that we feel intensely the limits, emptiness, and negativity of living, while positive and fulfilling meaning in life seems to be distant, foreign, and almost unreal. As a result, we sense that we really don't matter much to anyone or to ourselves. Life feels like a line of zeroes adding up to nothing.[1] T.S. Eliot calls it "waiting without hope."[2] Simone Weil's conclusion is that "the soul knows for certain only that it is hungry."[3] In this state, death is emptiness in the form of an event. Although we try to hide this state behind our cultural obsession with "youth," and by closeting off the elderly in "care" facilities, the struggle of *being* and *nonbeing* is operative everywhere. The day I "knew," knew that "I knew," was a wind-swept November evening, as I looked down on the bleak valley of my birth, surrounded by black hills of rubble from the mines, from the vantage point of the cemetery.

4. Modern Life and the Desert

Several years ago on a flight from Los Angeles, I sat next to the editor of a magazine for bowling alley owners. She was returning from a conference. "What do folks like that have to conference about?" "The big one now is what video games to permit in our alleys." I was interested, so she continued. "Remember when you were a kid, the rage was pinball machines." I agreed, sharing with her the day I won fifty free games. "Games today are alarmingly different. A kid is enclosed in a black box. Not only does she or he play the 'game' alone, but does so knowing that she or he can *never* win. The contest, instead, is to see how long one can hold 'them' off before they get you." Somewhere over Reno, I sank into heavy thought. Apparently for youth today death is simply a matter of time. And as their inevitable future, it will always be premature; So the "how soon" is hardly an issue. This observation helps to make sense of the tragic school shootings. Whether one's hurts are of the smaller or larger variety is of little import. From personal slighting to social rejection, from ridicule to racial hatred, to the absoluteness of a nuclear holocaust, these become so intermingled that school violence may simply be a suicidal act of making one's own death matter—if only by the size of the body count. To live in such a world is to live in the "desert."

Yes, we all live in the desert "east of Eden," where birth and death merge as primal expressions of exile. Beginnings and endings, breadth and height, time and timelessness—all these constitute the primal dimensions of one's time and space, and they are being drained of meaning each day. Personal, cultural, historical, cosmic time, once with deep senses of rich consummation—these are largely gone in our society. The Church's Sacraments and sacramental acts, the radiance of matter in a transforming of space—these too are pathetically "garbaged," as they have no meaning for many people. Instead, so many live in the clutter of an isolated intersection called the "present." To live as persons without history is to be an endangered species, for the present becomes the thinnest of lines separating "not yet" and "too late."

I found an interesting phenomenon in the local weekly newspaper. The paper is a harbinger of a time past, for it still reports who visited whom this week and what they had for dessert. But two things have changed. First, the sheriff's report no longer indicates how many cats have been rescued from trees this week. Instead, drug labs and drug sales are frequent now. Second, in a village priding itself on its tradition, more and more obituary notices indicate cremation, *without any service.* Even here, then, in the Ozark Hills, many of the dead no longer have a special place, for their time is arbitrary. The mortician told me that the "disposal" of the ashes is usually left to him, to be scattered whenever and wherever the mortician finds convenient. He uses them to fertilize his roses.

More deeply now than perhaps at any other time in its history, the Church is at a crossroads. Its viability rests in its ability to provide an alternative way of living time and space than that which characterizes our bitter age, an age of materialism and individualism. Put graphically, Christianity is finished if it is unable to provide an alternative way of life—an alternative to the sweeping conquest of secular capitalism. This would require the understanding and power sufficient to re-sacralize time and space—with their intersecting establishing the "mystery" of place.

But our crisis is even deeper. A prior task for the Church is to rediscover the identity of her *own* pilgrimage. The Gospel of Mark identifies it in the words of Jesus himself: "The time is fulfilled, and the kingdom of God has come near; repent, and believe in the good news" (Mark 1:15). Immediately thereafter, Jesus called his disciples for one task—that of the Kingdom, which is the common-wealth, the reign of God. Jesus touches a dream deep within each of us, of a "where" and a "when," personal and social, in which space and time so intersect that a "field of dreams" emerges as a promise. This seemingly impossible hope wraps itself around the "where" and "when" that God shall create a new earth, adorned as a bride for her husband, in which the Incarnation of God with us shall be forever. And this God, the Alpha becoming Omega, will give water to the thirsty without price; and will wipe away every tear from [our] eyes, and death shall be no more (Rev. 21:1-4).

I don't know any man who did not cry, even sob, during the motion picture *Field of Dreams*. The reconciliation between father and son was a transcending of the "then" and "there" by the "here" and "now." In this drama, the resolution is held together by the symbol of play—catching a ball together, for its own sake, in a timeless moment. The Christian in particular should be able to understand this— time is timeless, at a special place that is everywhere. "In the fullness of time," we become "no longer slave or free," but heirs who will "inherit the Kingdom of God." (Gal. 4:4; 3:28; 4:5; 5:21). I sobbed because although my father played professional baseball, I don't ever remember him even tossing and catching a ball with me.

The "Garden of Eden" is God's ongoing activity of creation and re-creation, into which God calls us humans to be co-gardeners. We, in turn, are to lure and cajole forth, with God, the beauty of a joyous consummation of time and space. Jesus' promise of the "Kingdom" is a pilgrimage of the timeless in time and the spaceless within space. It is one of divine beginnings and endings, as time intersects with space as revelation. To *be,* the Christian anatomy for both self and history must be in decided contrast to the everyday world of domesticated secularism.

5. Solitude and the Sacredness of Place

As a boy, I had a special place that was my own "private spot." Each of my friends had their own place—a tree house, a large rock down by the river, the hayloft. While on rare occasions one might share the sacred place with a special friend, all of us understood the unspoken "rule":

"Visitation" was by invitation only. My own secure place was under our low front porch, behind the lattice. The place smelled of earth. Here I could cry; here the blemishes of time were cleansed and a balance of perspective returned. Here my imagination was given free play: for a toy car I could create endless roads and dirt castles. It was a magic place, one of make-believe. I learned early that this was a place not to be shared. I knew that if I did, there would be a point when my "friend" would squeal, and with a stick find delight in knocking down all that we had made. Although later in my young years I had a favorite maple-tree limb from which to view the world that I would soon try to change, under the porch always remained my "special place."

During that time I was not conscious of any parallel, but now I realize my own special sacred place was in reality a search for a "womb" that would resonate with the trek of our ancient ancestors. In southern France, one can still feel the sacredness of the dark and silent deep of womblike caves. Powerful is the experience of standing inside the Great Pyramid, deep in its silent center, a place so sacred that it was tightly sealed against time itself, destined to be for Eternity. Space of all spaces, with the Time of all times. Such examples are so legion that one begins to sense the profound yearning of all humankind for special locations, sacred spaces—hidden and unavailable, secret and intimate—*where time stands at attention.*

Trappist monasteries, such as mine, are placed in the most remote, wild, solitary places. And yet, we are sought out and found, our guest houses filling almost to over-flowing. Our rule of life is more than 1,500 years old, and our singing is Gregorian chant, which is almost as old. We call forth the saints from all of time to surround us with Mystery. Ours is a life lived as it was, and is, and will keep being. In our own way, monasteries serve much as did the sacred caves. In many of the caves are timeless drawings, which convey the power of spirit in the embodiment of animals with which our ancestors most identified. And in the profound stillness of the tombs, incredible paintings cover the walls and often the ceilings. When one gazes on these, time stops. It is as if offering up sacramental gifts to Eternity fulfills time. Deep in all humans there seems to be a struggle and a call so to sacralize space with time that with the stroke of a brush, space is rendered timeless, and time becomes spaceless. This calling is a life enterprise.

I would even venture that the ugly tendency to carve one's own name at sacred places is rooted in an unconscious sense of one's own fragile time. It is as if we need to make a claim to something that can outlast one's own finite self—if only in graffiti. I remember not long ago stopping in awe, when before me stood a huge tree, with the year 1867 carved on its trunk. There it was, while the anonymous carver is now dust in some unweeded plot.

The Yucatan ruins grasp me deeply, with their seemingly endless steps reaching skyward, to a small, remote temple hung high above the surrounding jungle. At the doorway, looking back, I can feel something of the mystery that I felt when dreaming as a boy. Sitting on my tree limb on a gentle summer morning, the breeze mesmerizing me with its swaying, I remembered that all was centered and all was well.

I imagine all children have a cigar box (or its equivalent) hidden under their bed. The contents are of little value, yet they have the ability to symbolize the child's identity. My box had my favorite marble I used for special games as a "shooter," a diagram of how to build different kinds of kites, and a slingshot. When I grew older, it contained a special stone from the top of the first serious mountain I climbed, a ticket stub from game seven when the Royals took the Cards in the World Series. Maybe others have a lock of hair from the girl who sat behind them in school— the one still loved.

So it was with ancient Israel, who laid claim to Mystery through an "Ark of the Covenant." The Ark was profoundly honored, whether within its special tent in the desert, or the rich confines of the later Temple of Solomon. Yet it functioned much like a corporate cigar box. There wasn't anything of value in it, really. But *that* object in *that* place was the very meaning of Israel's time. Open it if you dare. Inside there actually wasn't much, not much at all. There were two rough stones, roughly carved as a basis for the Ten Commandments. There was a stick, said to be Aaron's staff. And strangest of all was a small vessel holding that mysterious stuff said to be manna. That's it. The Temple where it was housed had a courtyard, with the aroma of animal flesh from the "altar of burnt sacrifice." Nearby was a table of shewbread and a laver of water for purification, moving the worshiper's attention forward toward the high "altar of incense."

The rites appropriate for these special places, collectively called the "Holy Place," were preliminary to the Mystery within mysteries, a space set aside as the "Holy of Holies." This was the very dwelling place of God, for this was where the Ark was housed. It was so special that to touch it was to risk death, and its Mystery was so intense that this Holy Place could be entered only once each year, for incensing—

33

by a priest chosen specially by God, through the casting of lots. That Infinite Mystery is bottomless.

With the destruction of this Temple in A.D. 70, however, meaning for the Jews could no longer be centered in participation in that Mystery. Rather, Jewish ceremonies became practices observed in the home, with emphasis on the synagogue for times of prayer and the reading and explication of Scripture. This destruction of the Temple occurred at the very time that first-generation Christians were struggling to make sense of their "crucified Messiah." As one might expect, this tragedy of the Temple played an important part in Christians' coming to understand the fuller meaning of the Christ event. The Letter to the Hebrews, written near the time of the Temple's destruction, is the longest sustained argument of any book of the Bible. The formative image is that Christ, as God, is both sacrifice and priest in the once-and-for-all ceremony of the Eucharist, which we are to offer constantly as "the sacrifice of praise."

6. Dual Traditions of Word and Altar

A traditional way of understanding different strands in Christian history is to see in St. Paul's letters the good news of the *Word,* rooted in the prophets, centering in justification by grace through faith, focused upon evangelization of the Gentiles. In contrast stands St. Peter, the first Bishop of Rome, standing in the lineage of the priests, whose tradition is sacramentally inclined. The Protestant Reformers, offended deeply by misuses within the sacramental tradition, rediscovered in St. Paul's writings the avenue for recovering the gospel through "proclamation of the Word." Appropriately, three major Protestant thinkers—Martin Luther, John Wesley, and Karl Barth—began powerful reforms through discovering the gospel in a powerful way through St. Paul's Letter to the Romans.

Roman Catholicism, on the other hand, has steadfastly preserved something of the Temple's anatomy and mystery. In every Catholic Church there is a "sanctuary": a raised place set aside for the sacrifice to be celebrated on an altar. In further analogy with the Jewish Temple, there is within this sacramental demarcation a "tabernacle," covered with a "veil." It is torn in half, as was the Temple veil when Christ died, as himself the "Holy of Holies."

As far back as we can go in church history, an important task for the priest was to give *viaticum*—food for the journey of the dying. When I went away to college, my mother gave me lunch in a brown paper sack to eat on the bus. So it is for the Christian nearing death. The sacramental Body of Christ is given as food for one's final trek. In those early days, death came on its own terms, with little medical capacity to delay the inevitable. Thus there was an urgent need to have consecrated "hosts" available, intentionally left over from the previous Eucharist. These needed to be kept somewhere deserving of respect, with a lighted candle indicating that, mysteriously, they are not simply what they look like, but what they really are. These are housed inside the tabernacle in a *ciborium,* a vessel resembling a chalice with a lid. It functions much like the Ark, for in it is nothing of empirical value, not really— only some flour-and-water disks. And yet, in this "little" is the presence of the "much"—the "Real Presence" of God with us—for just as the Spirit infused Mary, so the Spirit promises to infuse these simple gifts of bread and wine. This mystery is the timeless ongoingness of the Incarnate God, through whom at the Eucharist we participate in the divine action of Crucifixion, Resurrection, and Ascension. In this holy space, through this holy action, all of time stands still; for in this intersection of time with space is disclosed the very being of "God with us"—the timeless One who is and was and ever shall be the Lord of time.

However this sacralization of time and space is understood and practiced, the Church is the Body of "Christ," fed by the Eucharist as the "Body" of Christ. The word *temple* means both a "dwelling place" and an "inner sanctuary." Thus just as the Church is God's "dwelling place," so is each Christian an "inner sanctuary," a "temple of the Holy Spirit" (1 Corin. 6:19). Within both is a "soul," which is the "Holy of Holies." Undergirding this understanding is a deep sense of continuity—for the sacredness of life is a mystery of growth in each temporal stage of its development. And it is through Communion that we ourselves become a continuation of the Incarnation.

Some years ago, as I struggled for an analogy through which I could better understand who God really is, my spiritual director said simply, "Receive the 'Body of Christ' at Communion and then let that reality sweep over you in thankfulness. What happens as incarnation in you is the mystery of Jesus Christ as the disclosure of who God is, and what God is doing—everywhere." This is also what it means to believe that the Incarnate God known in history as Jesus Christ takes up "residence" in the sacred space of the Church as "Real Presence." This sacramental life is no mere repetition of a past event, for Christ's sacrifice is once and

36

for all. Nor is the Eucharist simply an illustration of the proclaimed Word. Jesus Christ is the *primal disclosure of the name, nature, and activity of God*. Such a revelation, then, is far more than a revelation of what God did two millennia ago in the thirty-three-year period of Jesus' earthly life. In the Eucharist, *time folds in upon itself*, rendering holy the particular space of its happening. If the Christ event is the revelation of the very nature of God, then what God did in the temporal aperture of Christ's life is a disclosure of what God did, does, and will do—forever. This is who God is.

It is in the dynamic of the Eucharist, then, that we participate in this ongoing incarnation of God, formed in time as the dramatic rhythm of *Crucifixion-Resurrection-Ascension*. Put another way, Christ's promise in the *past* invites us in the *present* to participate as foretaste of our *future* with God. In the Eucharist, both past and future enter the present as *Mystery*. God is present not only in the Eucharist, but also in the various Sacraments that appear at each of the "hinge points" in life's pilgrimage. The Sacraments address the prebirth needs and deep cravings persisting from childhood, and each Sacrament is like a final puzzle piece placed in the empty place where only it can fit.

Just as the Sacraments make contact with the anatomy of our *birthing* process, so they also bring clarity to the image of "Holy Mother Church." The Church is not primarily an organization. In reality, it is our Mother who gives new birth to us, as Mary gave birth to Christ.[4] Given this significance, one can understand why Christians through the ages have used gestures of reverence to acknowledge the *Mystery* that is the Church, binding together the altar, the lectern, the tabernacle, the Scripture, and the presider, who acts "in the person of Christ."

Protestantism tends to focus upon the image of "hearing." Catholicism prefers to focus upon the image of "seeing." Both are needed.

7. Mystery as Intersection

One could certainly make a case that our culture, to its detriment, is intentionally devoid of Mystery. In strong contrast, the Church through the centuries has manifested its own profound sense of Mystery. This is true not only through its Sacraments, but by building monasteries in which life as Mystery can be pursued deeply for its own sake. Before Vatican II, the immediate family of "candidates" for the monastic life (male or female) could accompany them only as far as the huge oak doors, which read "Monastic Enclosure—No Admittance." There the family said their farewells, knowing that a person passing through those doors "died" to all but Christ. Pictures, treasured tokens, everything that would remind the potential monk or nun of his or her "previous life," were returned. With nothing except the clothes one was wearing, he or she would enter the monastic enclosure, never to see or be seen by the outside world again. The only exit was by death—but even then only to the backyard.

Beyond the doors, one's hair would be cut, symbolizing that there, with no mirrors, one forfeits all concern for "appearance." Then a time would come when one was sufficiently prepared to lie prostrate before the abbot or abbess. Covered symbolically by the black cloth of death, one died to self. When asked what one wanted, one offered one's whole life to the monastic community as an organic

38

part of the Body of Christ. In arising, one did so as a new person with new clothing within a new "world." Before being embraced by each member of the community, the new monk or nun was given a new name—that of the saint in whose footsteps one was called to follow.

However this monastic way of life might be understood, *Mystery* is affirmed by monasteries as the fundamental nature of Christian living. *Life itself is mystery* and marks us deeply, whether we experience it in birth or death, calling or rejection, friendship or marriage. What makes everything different for the Christian is not so much *what* is added or subtracted from one's living. What makes life different is that one's *attitude* toward everything is transfigured— one's "disposition of the heart and . . . frame of mind" is best understood as "the relation of loved to loved one."[5] And in living at this beveled edge between spirit and world, the monastic lives on the frontier of meaning. The chalice offered at the Eucharist is, above all, the invitation to drink deeply of the mystery that lies in front, above, under, within, and beyond us. Likewise, all Sacraments identify the intersections of time and space where God has promised to act, not exclusively, but intensively.

8. Monasticism and the Christian Family

We will have occasions to refer to monasteries, for through the centuries the Church has recognized, recruited, and nurtured those who were called to live the Christian life in an intense and absolute kind of way. When Martin Luther came to Worms to defend himself, he was still dressed as an Augustinian monk. In time he came to affirm that this complete way of living the faith was intended for all persons, not simply the "special." His way of symbolizing this belief was to marry and have a family. This meant that Luther transferred his focus and allegiance from the monastery to the "Christian family." This was to be the heart of faithfulness, enabling the family to serve as a model for all Christians. With the present crisis in the "institution" of family, it might be wise to look seriously at monasteries as the organism from which the modern family was birthed.

In significant contrast to our intensely mobile society, a Trappist monk vows to spend his whole life living in and loving one particular place. In the midst of particular brothers or sisters, he or she learns the secrets and stories stored in the creaking, time-saturated monastic walls, greets each living thing in the woods and meadows by name, and walks the contours of the land recognized as sacred, season after season. In becoming able to know the *place* of one's stability as if it were one's own body, *horizontal time* takes on another complexion. Everything becomes perceived as circular, turning slowly around a divine axis—as T.S. Eliot put it, the "still point" of time's turning wheel in a "pattern of timeless moments."[6] The monk is given life one day at a time, to be returned each night with "confession" and "interest." Each day within each week within each year is, in one sense, fundamentally like the years of the past and like those yet to come. These moments compose each lifetime within a Mystery of likeness. Yet such life is like Chinese puzzle boxes, each set within each—until with the final one, the set forms a whole, all centered in each other.

I recently saw two monks arguing about what year it

was. It turned out that both were wrong—if the calendar is of value. Monastic life is a powerful countercultural community, as life in a new time intersects a new space and day by day life is marinated in Mystery.

9. Sacraments and Prebirth

Whether we refer to the seven Sacraments authorized by the Catholic Church or the two Protestant Sacraments plus "ordinances," a central reason for the Church's existence is *to enable the Spirit to intersect at the temporal hinge points of human life.* The Sacraments begin as acts that touch deeply one's prebirth formation. Baptism, Confirmation, and Eucharist are called the "Sacraments of initiation." The emerging infant, surrounded and enfolded by fluid within the womb, is birthed now into the arms of Holy Mother Church, as it were. Thus the baby is baptized soon, because through Baptism one receives adoption into a new "organism"—the womb of "Holy Mother Church" and the "Body of Christ."

The pulsing air in the maternal lungs of prebirth now finds its parallel in the Holy Spirit's taking residence within the "new" self. The Gospel of John masterfully illustrates this. Just as Genesis portrays the self as being created when God breathes life into the clay-formed body, so after the Resurrection, Jesus "breathed on [the disciples] and said to them, 'Receive the Holy Spirit'" (John 20:22). Just as the prebirth child is fed directly from the body of the mother, from her very flesh and blood, so it is spiritually. "Holy Mother Church" feeds us at the breast, as it were, in the Eucharist—and so direct is this feeding that it makes

41

sense to call this relationship one of "Real Presence." It is significant that in older times after Baptism the person was given milk and honey to drink.

Through this spiritual birthing process, the advent of consciousness begins in the child, casting each human being on a pilgrimage as he or she moves increasingly toward self-consciousness. It is this natural process that the Church makes sacred by intersecting it with the Spirit in the Sacrament of Confirmation. In this sacramental event, the self is sealed by the Spirit in a grace-filled present, in which the promises made for one in the past become the promises now made by oneself and give shape to one's future. Andre Louf wisely says of this redemptive pilgrimage that it "is like breathing, like the heartbeat of the world, the expression of its deepest longing for salvation and healing."[7] In this "coming of age," the Christian begins to discern that one's pilgrimage takes place in the valley between Eden and the Kingdom, between Advent and Epiphany, between Lent and Pentecost. And in living within these antinomies, one comes to recognize that each of us is a *homo viator,* a wanderer. One's defining rhythm is discerned by recognizable events of intersection. To help us, the Church provides Sacraments as markers for the trail.

In spite of this deep correlation between the primal human cravings and the sacramental invitations of the Church, both child and adult are tempted to find their own way. What we seek is to escape the gnawing emptiness deep within—vacant, barren, blank, bare, lurking. We can attempt escape in one or both of two ways. First is the temptation to control one's *space* with possessions—stuffing every corner, piling up exponential ownership against the inevitable demise, even though no one can take anything with them. I remember, as a child, owning ninety-six marbles, proudly housed and hidden in a big glass jar. Each week I would count them. But I never took any to school, for I could not take the chance of playing marbles during recess for fear of losing some, even one. It isn't too large a jump from such an obsession to an adult's attempt to find remedies for anxiety. A favorite solution is to acquire a larger house than needed, in order to store things. And a favorite interim plan is to displace the cars from the garage, until the garage is so junked by "stuff" that the thought of having "empty space" is humorous. To us comes God's attention-grabber: "Fool! This very night your life is being demanded of you" (Luke 12:20).

There is a second way to seek escape from our finitude. We call it "time management." Are there any middle-class, middle-aged Americans who do not feel overwhelmed by all they feel obligated to do? Symptomatic of the state of our lives, workshops in "time management" have sprung up everywhere. Intent upon escaping any sense of guilt for being who we are and living as we live, we learn ever-new techniques for stuffing one's time beyond capacity. In this effort, the passage toward nonbeing becomes strewn with palm leaves of overtime.

These ways of coping with this societal dynamic of "having" and "doing" identify the degree to which our pulsating "center" or "soul" is in profound tension. On one hand, deep within, is a *boundless* craving to lose consciousness in a surrogate womb simulating one's inception. On the other hand, is the yearning for *boundaries*, for closure, for some sort of consummation that can flow back meaningfully over the whole, much as ends relate to means. Expressed in terms befitting one's Christian

43

pilgrimage, living is like hanging over the chasm between innocence and consummation. *Innocence* characterizes the desire to lose one's self by returning to the Source—into Being Itself. This yearning is for timeless space, for a mystic state before any disjoining of self and Other—either in the womb or in the state before the beginning of history itself. *Consummation,* on the other hand, is a sallying forth, equipped only with a Promise, intent upon the fulfillment of self and Kingdom.

When one loses one's innocence, however, as inevitably occurs, there is really no way back. An angel guards the gate of Eden (Gen.3:24). Driven out of the garden, each of us becomes like Abraham, going out but "not knowing where [one is] going" (Heb. 11:8). As "strangers and foreigners on the earth . . . [we] are seeking a homeland . . . a better country" (Heb. 11:13-14, 16). Faith, as "the assurance of things hoped for" (Heb. 11:1), means living under promise, having tasted the flavor of what is to be. Yet we must live content to "know" by sampling time at the edges of our yearnings. Inside, our souls are like chalice's for God's gentle pouring. And outside, we pour our doings into the world as God's chalice. In the fall, early each morning, I look out from the vantage of a special monastic window. My yearning within is moved by a dense frothy fog without, making a eucharist of the valley. It is enough.

10. Sexuality and the Human Craving

It is almost universal that those exploring the nature of religion in general and Christianity in particular acknowledge that the beginning of spiritual awareness is integrally tied to a profound sense of need, experienced as craving. Merton insists that it is an insatiable thirsting that lets God come within us. In turn, probably the most powerful craving and thirst in human life is *sexuality*. Indeed, this powerful craving, characterizing as well animal and plant life, would seem to extend even to microorganisms. This drive is composed of two contrasting dimensions. On the one hand, is the *expansive* drive: to thrust into conception, to force upon, to consume from. Approaching animality, this drive can bring one to acts of violent subduing. Fecundity issues from every particle of nature, as if God's command drives all things to "be fruitful and multiply, and fill the earth and subdue it" (Gen. 1:28). The second dimension, perhaps unique to humans, is a craving for the ecstasy of losing oneself in another—a drive for *inclusivity,* as the joyous intersection of spirit and flesh.

Sigmund Freud identified this sexuality permeating all human activity as the *libido,* meaning "longing." Although he identified this second dimension of sexuality, he lacked the experience himself and thus was unable to deal with it. He called it the "oceanic feeling," the "desire for oneness with the universe," the uniting of ego and world, much as when one is in love. It is the "sensation of 'eternity,' a feeling as of something limitless, unbounded—as it were, 'oceanic.'" This is the mystery in which to "lose oneself."[8] Freud also recognized this second dimension as the source of religious energy. But once again, failing to discover this feeling in himself, he regarded it as illusion. At other times, Freud identified religion as endless wishing—and that for which one wishes is never to be abandoned, homeless, or outcast. As a result, that which is most deadly is when society, or those closest to a person, renders one

45

unwilling or unable to wish any more. As a result, one is no longer able to pay attention to one's dreams and hopes, and therefore is incapable of listening to one's heart.

For Christian spirituality, both dimensions of sexuality are necessary as alternations between separation and union. This sexuality of spirituality insists upon a way of life in which both the spiritual and carnal intermingle—for example, through prayer and dancing, the kiss of the Eucharist and the passion of one's loins, sobriety and inebriation, contemplation and action, Gregorian chant and sensual music, engaging God in embrace and in struggle. "I love because I love," said St. Bernard, for to fall madly in love with God is to want nothing more than to be lost forever in the ecstasy. Although Protestant theology rarely deals with such matters, Protestant hymnology is filled with this vision of God. "Changed from glory into glory, . . . till we cast our crowns before thee, lost in wonder, love, and praise."[9] "Breathe on me, Breath of God, till I am wholly thine, till all this earthly part of me glows with thy fire divine."[10] It is through the analogy of sex that one can sense the nature of one's final relation with God: to be ravished and consumed.

On the other hand, our sexuality is expressive of the divine drive toward completion—in ourselves, in others, and in creation. Here we find a basic irony. The deeper one moves into this passion for completion, the more intense our yearning is to lose ourselves in the Eternal Lover. The sexuality of spirituality rests on the wager that the sexual yearning deep within us is, in truth, our longing for God. If only for a moment, our doing and our being embrace as a divine-human love affair. Then it is that we may finally realize, as Ernest Becker said in *The Denial of God,* that

God is the only adequate sex partner. And it was St. Bernard, in turn, who insisted that it is only grace that can sublimate this libido into divine-human creativity.

11. The Givenness of God

These dual relations rooted in sexuality undergird the contrast between the contemplative and apostolic. Both Hinduism and Buddhism stress surrendering one's life into Nothingness—returning, as it were, into the primal womb of the cosmos. Here time is forfeited for mystical "space" in the eternal now. While Christian mystics explore this dimension fruitfully, they agree that the contemplative experience must not eliminate the semblance of relationship—for God and self are not identical. Thus in the experience of "oneness" with one's Source, there is always a "before" that implies an "after"—for in all things, God is prior.

This means that *for the Christian, time and space are both real and vital*, rendered profoundly sacred in their intersections. Time intersects space as "event," and space intersects time as "history." Above all, it is Christ's Incarnation that declares time and space to be real and thus discloses that all is immersed in God's becoming. Thus while Christians can be grasped deeply by immersion in the Source, it is equally necessary to affirm Christian spirituality as being grasped eschatologically by creation. That is, everything that *is* is also "becoming," *rendered so by Promise.* Jesus Christ is our basis for insisting that history is real, actual, and central to the "ways of the Lord."

Thus the Christian affirms the *temporal* nature of

47

space, and the *spatial* nature of time. While the Hindu or Buddhist seeks to return to the primal womb through a denial of space and time, Christians struggle toward the "consummation" of all time and space. This refers to a "Kingdom" that is now but not yet, present but still to come, promised but not actual—yet impregnating every present. It is within this tension that life emerges as pilgrimage, as we seek meaning through the sacralizing of time and space, with their intersection understood as revelation. "Then" and "when" intersect as "now"—contingent upon the forward edge of the past, anticipating the future as hospitable stranger, in an ongoing depth as the Present.

CHAPTER THREE

Time and Space as Relationship

"My soul thirsts for God." (Ps.42:2)
"There is nothing on earth that I desire other than you." (Ps.73:25)
"Your steadfast love is better than life." (Ps.63:3)

1. Time and Space as Real

Space does not exist without objects, nor objects without space. And time exists only if that which does exist can be characterized as in a state of "becoming." Thus everything that is exists within a relationship. This is true of value as well. When we say something is of value, we mean that it is valuable *for* something or someone. This relational understanding, however, produced significant difficulties for medieval theologians. Many followed Aristotle in insisting that since God is the "fullness of being," there can be no change or *becoming* in God; thus time does not exist for God. In addition, since the perfect is unchanging in every way, it is impossible for God to know the world directly, for it is constantly in flux. The only way that Aquinas found for inserting the Creator God of Christianity into this Aristotelian scheme was to claim that God eternally and timelessly knows all things. But this posed another issue. How, then, can there be any freedom to become within the world, without which time is an illusion?

Other theologians followed Plato's lead. His analogy was that we live in a cave, facing a far wall, on which we see projected only the shadows of things as they pass before the sun at the mouth of the cave. Doomed to this state, we never see anything directly. When awakened, however, we turn toward the light, perceiving things as they are essentially, rooted in the eternal forms that themselves are unmoving and unchanging.

In either approach, however, time and space are less than real. Thus, although these two primary philosophical options have had great influence on Christian theologians, they seem to stand in contradiction to two basic biblical tenets. First, since the God of Scripture is the Creator of all things, that which God created must be regarded as real. Second, the God of Scripture is one of gracious compassion, who, while capable of anger, offers newness of life in such a way that humans may reject it. Yet the problem persists. If God must await our response to God's invitation, God's knowledge would be imperfect—for it involves God in time. Whatever option is taken, the only way out that medieval theologians could see was to affirm some form of predestination or foreknowledge. In that way, God's knowledge could be eternal and thus unchanging. But if the Christian, nevertheless, continues to insist on time and space being quite real because God created them, the only apparent answer they knew was to understand time, and thus history, as *circular.* Even though Scripture seems to take a linear view of history, to affirm this, they figured, would force us to affirm that real change happens, and thus draw what for them was the unacceptable conclusion that God's knowledge changes.

I remember only too well a heated argument that

neo-Thomist Jacque Maritain and I had while we both taught at Princeton. Maritain contended that the Kingdom of God that *will be* is actually a return to the Garden of Eden that *once was.* Thus since history is the result of the fall, it has no real status in being. And because history cannot add anything to God, history cannot go anywhere except back to the original state of God's creation, before human sin began history. This rendered time, ultimately, as unreal, being only that which is destined to be overcome by God.

As I listened to Maritain on that gray November day, there seemed to be something terribly immoral about such an understanding. I refused to concede to any system in which the struggle and agony of time, and thus history, would finally be as naught. All the heartache, the pain, the suffering, the importance of genius, the works of art, the blood of the martyrs—all of this to be destined for the dumpster? For me, that would render time and history hopelessly insane. God would only bring us back to "Go," without even two hundred fake dollars to make the "game" a bit more palatable. Actually, it would be worse than that. This return to the beginning would be totally God's doing, in no way the result of our actions or even our lives. Such "logic" erupts with perhaps the heaviest question of all: *If God will eventually take over the reins, how can a God be so cruel as to wait until we make a complete tragedy of ourselves?*

While some of these philosophical systems have led Christian understandings down some questionable paths, so have certain Christian mystics. Mystics tend to regard time and space as unreal, for they are distractions from the total unity of pure spirit. I remember one particular warning that St. John of the Cross gave as an illustration of how persons of prayer should act when in the quietness of a cave. Do not, under any circumstances, he insisted, touch the damp moss on the cave's ceiling. Sensuality is a distraction. In contrast, my understanding of Christian spirituality *insists* that one should touch it, stroke it, and give thanks for the soft, gentle, greenness of such a gem in God's creation. And yet John of the Cross's negative advice follows necessarily from his understanding that since "becoming" and all growth occurs in time, and that which is real is Eternal, the earth is a major distraction. In mystical experience, all is One, without distinctions of separateness. It follows as well that one's reason or mind is a distraction, necessitating a "mantra" to occupy it so as to keep it out of the way of one's contemplative life.

Rather than holding to a view of the nontemporal nature of "reality," the Christian spirituality that we are exploring maintains that *the relational character of everything constitutes value.* Nothing is objective, independent of perception. Color does not exist for the color-blinded. Furthermore, when we see a magnificent sunset, we crave to show it to someone else. Short of that, we store up adjectives we ache to share. Likewise, gold is of value only if some people want it, whatever their reason. If relationship is fundamental, it follows that whatever is perceived relates significantly to the uniqueness of the person who beholds it. And relationship depends not only on who a person is in one's unique pilgrimage, but also on where that person stands in order to see. Thus *authentic* time is not that which is measured chronologically in terms of hours, minutes, and seconds. Rather, time adheres to the nature of a particular experience. Who is to say that time spent making love is equivalent to the same exact "amount" of time spent in a dentist chair? No one, except those obsessed with a ticking gadget. "Time flies" is a familiar saying, referring to "desirable" experiences, as is "where did the time go!" On the other hand, "I thought it would never end" is the emotional expression for how time seems to drag when one wants only to finish the task. Boredom reflects the tedium of time at its slowest, for one has no interest in what is going on.

For the Christian, then, *chronos* as "measured sequence" is swallowed up in *kairos*, meaning a fullness of time. *Kairos* is a Greek word for time-space experienced as pregnant with meaning. St. Paul understood this difference when he wrote of Christ coming in "the fullness of time" (Gal. 4:4) or "when the time had fully come."

2. Scripture and Perspective

It seems that in every generation some scholars try one more time to do a "quest for the historical Jesus." Each new effort tries some "technique" for determining which "facts" are *objectively* true about Jesus. Albert Schweitzer's classic book, *The Quest for the Historical Jesus,* came to a sobering conclusion. Christ comes to each of us as one unknown. All efforts to know Jesus as he "truly" was end up saying far more about the perceiver conducting the search than the one about whom one is searching.

Thus not only is value relational, but so is knowledge. H. R. Niebuhr said it well when he insisted that all "believing takes place in this social context of believing companions whom we trust. Selves are social knowers living in covenant relations."[1] Thus one cannot know what Jesus *really* said, or what he *really* did, and who as a matter of fact he *really* was. All we can know are what appear to be answers to such questions as seen from the differing perspectives of different persons. So it is with *all* of our knowing. Suppose, for example, I want to know who my cousin Jack *really* is. I ask his wife—and she tells me who he is *for her*. Then I ask friends who sing with him in the choir on Sunday. That "he has a good tenor voice" doesn't relate much to his wife's appraisal that "he is a good lover." Nor do any of these surmises relate in any helpful way to what his drinking buddies at the neighborhood bar have to say about him. Even his own children have diverse perspectives on their "growing up" with dad.

Well, then, let's go straight to Jack himself. Surely he knows. "Jack, who are you, really?" What can he say? Often the individual is the one least likely truly to know one's own self. So Jack, in the end, turns out to be a composite of the relationships he has, and even could have, and how "he" perceives the "him" in these. But all these perspectives are a matter of hunches based on the contingencies of relationships. If Jack dies, and someone writes a biography of him, when they interview me I can remember some things Jack said, but not precisely. And when asked various questions about him, I would feel free to say not what he *actually* did or said, but what would have been consistent for him to have said or done on certain occasions.

Such is the case with the Gospel writers. All depends on who is doing the "seeing" and where that person stands to see, as determined by the needs that characterize that person's particular pilgrimage. More than this is impossible.

Yet the impossibility of these various quests for the *real* Jesus is not of major concern to the Christian. So-called "objectivity," even if there is such a thing, is outside the realm of the Christian's vital interest. What is valuable is the testimony of persons who, in one form or another, can say, as did the blind man, "I do not know whether he is a sinner. One thing I do know, that though I was blind, now I see" (John 9:25). Jesus himself emphasized such knowing when he asked his disciples, Who do people say that I am? Then he asked, "But who do *you* say that I am?" (Matt. 16:13, 15; emphasis added).

That is *the* question of interest to the Christian. When many persons left Jesus, he turned to Simon Peter: "Do you also wish to go away?" The response makes all the difference: "Lord, to whom can we go? You have the words of eternal life" (John 6:67-68). The concern for Christians is not to seek to know, in some objective sense, who Jesus was, for such knowledge is impossible. The issue is *who he is for me.* This is a relationship called faith. The Church should not be particularly interested in more studies or in additional instructions for selling the gospel. The concern should be with "salvation seeing"—with what H.R. Niebuhr calls "inner history," with participating in Biblical history from within.[2] "Neutrality" and "uncommitedness" he called the "great delusions."[3] All meaning is "resolutely confessional.[4] Thus Salvation occurs when the outer history pointed to in scripture becomes *my* history, within the Church where the Christ event is participated in as *our* history.[5] In fact, the uniqueness of the Church is its witness that through its sense of time seen as history, it knows where home is. It is in this sense that Ludwig Wittgenstein in his *Philosophical Investigations* called faith a "form of life."

55

For some time now, biblical scholars have been concerned with the contrasting perspectives of the four Gospel writers. Can their differences be unified? From the understanding we are developing, the answer is "no." The writers are indeed different, and that is precisely what we should expect and actually want. Our concern is with *healing*. The blindnesses and thus the needs of Matthew, Mark, Luke, and John are considerably different; so the transformed perspective by which each sees necessarily contrasts with that of the others. Instead of trying to find a least common denominator and attempting to unify the Jesus event, the Christian needs to glory in a plethora of names, images, similes, and metaphors. No amount of these can ever exhaust the time-space happening called the Christ event. Thus for the person of faith, B.C. and A.D. point to a marking that is profoundly real. They mark the "before" and the "after," the "question" and the "answer," the "once" and the "thence," in regard to which time becomes central.

But more is involved than this diversity of individual perspectives. Karl Marx, like Niebuhr, insisted that what one sees depends on those with whom one *corporately* stands. Marx struggled with this question: If truth is relational, with emphasis on the subjective pole of knowing, are there as many "truths" as there are people? His answer is "no," for he insists that truth depends on what is seen when one stands in a particular place—in his case with the proletariat. But why there? Marx somehow assumes that this perspective is "objective," constituting the very structure of time-space itself. In so saying, he identified what he called the dialectic of history itself, moving toward the perfect society. The Christian understands this differently. "Knowing" is always a risk-based faith. And the primal risk we must take is to identify where *God* has chosen to stand, providing *the* perspective by which Christians can see, know, and understand. The intersection of time and space provides us with a "when" and a "where" that together give us the "who." For example, liberation theologians wager that in the event of Jesus Christ, God has chosen to stand with the poor. Thus, they insist, the only way to understand everything and to see from God's perspective is to stand with the poor in their poverty.

H.R. Niebuhr identifies three different ways of knowing: wager, authority, and mystic immediacy. Yet the last two actually depend upon the first, and thus wager is unavoidable. What, then, determines the "truth" of our primal wagering? The "test" is the "livability" of the relationship(s) in which the conundrum of our human condition is addressed. The primal wager for the Christian is upon the sacredness of a *particularized* intersection of time with space. It is this intersection that provides us with the "from," "for," "with," and "to." Or again, in being addressed by the Christ event, we affirm that we are standing before God, with God, as God, and in God.

This wager on a particular intersection is not only that it happened "in the fullness of time," but indeed that it *was* the fullness of time. The Christian's task is to examine the multiple dimensions of time as they appear from the perspective of this particularized divine-human event in time. By entering history as a "when," God is declaring time to be real, and thus is *the* domain in which meaning occurs. All kinds of time are the arenas of God's life as well as ours. Karl Barth, in his *Dogmatics in Outline,* is so insistent that Christian life is living the richness of time that he eliminates entirely the image of "eternity," calling it inappropriate in speaking of God. The more accurate analogy, he claims, is to speak of "God's time," intersecting our time with a concrete name.

As a result, we will look for a particular primal image from which the Christian can understand and live the different kinds of *time*—cosmic, historical, life-span, yearly, monthly, weekly, daily, and momentary. And since time depends upon things for its existence, space exists only through the relationship of things. Thus, as we promised, we will focus upon Sacraments, sacramental acts, and ordinances as a way of perceiving how space is sacralized for the Christian. Throughout, it is important to keep sight of how God is to be understood in relationship to this sacralization. The key we will be exploring for establishing this perspective is *the need to make "Becoming," rather than "Being," a central category*. Our working premise will be that reality is shot through and through with the *present* as emergence from the *past*, and that at the far edge of the present is the *future*. This is so for us. It is so for God.

3. The Incarnation as Perspective

A central concern for the Christian, then, is *where* God chose to be "born." God could have been born as Herod, but he was born as a carpenter's son. He could have been born in a palace, but he deliberately chose a stable. He could have grown up in the "suburbs" of Jerusalem—with condo, indoor pool, and bridge tournaments every Friday. Yet he was born in Nazareth—a place totally remote, at the end of the road—a bit like Pumpkin Center, Kansas. Thus our theologizing perspective must operate by looking at society from the bottom up. This is the perspective not of the power elite; it is a unique perspective born near sulfur creeks, ancient graveyards, catacombs—anywhere outside the gate.

When Philip encountered Jesus, he was quick to share the experience with Nathanael. Nathanael's response was amazement: "Can anything good come out of Nazareth?" (John 1:43-46). His disdain was not simply for any *person* from Nazareth, but actually that any *thing* from Nazareth could be of any worth. Nazareth was the end of the line. As a youth, we who lived in South Fork had disdain for folks who lived across the creek in a town called Scoopie. But those folks didn't get depressed over the putdown, because the town down the railroad track was called "Scalp Level." Even this name was tolerable, because the crossroads at the end of the track was called "Turtle Creek." People there had no one to look down on. In Biblical times, Nazareth was the Turtle Creek of Palestine. The Christian perspective, then, is the one that emerges from a relationship between God and an unwed teenager of the lowest class from a backwater town. The witness is clear: The Incarnation occurred for the sake of losers, that they might become winners in a far different sense. The event called Jesus upset everything, if for no other reason than a primal promise that the first shall be last, and the rich shall become poor (Rev. 21:22f). It is as if the book of Revelation was meant as disaster relief for our own time.

This Christian perspective, rooted in a particular "wedding" of divine and human, was so intentional and profound that Jesus insisted that by befriending the poor we are actually and directly ministering to God—a God, it would seem, who is hungry, thirsty, a stranger, naked, and imprisoned (Matt. 25:31-40). The conclusion is important. *To stand with Christ at this concrete intersection of time with place is to understand God's compassionate choice in taking sides within our time.* In fact, there is good reason to wager that God *is* our time and our space—for it is *in* God that we live and move and have our being.

4. Creation and the *Imago Dei*

According to the Genesis account, God created humans in his own image and likeness. And who is that God? He is the one who had just thrown buckets full of stars skyward, delighted with the Milky Way that resulted. And at night, he is the one who played with the strange and exotic animals he had created. The image of God in which we are created, then, is that of the *Creator* God. Consequently, that which makes us "divine-like" is the creativity of our imagination, which, in turn, links us with the creative imagination of God. Incarnation is the explicit name for God's love affair with the time-space called Creation, and the way in which Creation shares in God. Seen through this Christian imagination, each and every thing begs to be completed—shaped, transformed, and released, aglow with the light streaming from the promise called future.

No wonder Annie Dillard in her *Pilgrim at Tinker's Creek* identified sin as a massive failure of imagination. In fact, imagination is so central for the Christian that one can identify the soul as its home base. Soul is the cave within, the womb, the chamber of one's heart, which one visits in one's imagination. To *create* and to *enjoy* the creation—these two traits express best the twin characteristics of both God and humans. The Creator calls us "to till [the Creation] and keep it" (Gen. 2:15) and to share with God the enjoyment of the Sabbath rest (Gen. 2:3). We are the gardeners not only of *space* but also of *time*, called as co-creators with God to "complete" history. Thomas Merton concurs when he identifies the *imago Dei* as being an artist/worker. Oscar Cullmann likewise describes each person as an artisan of a world in movement and the agent of a history in the process of being made. Andre Louf agrees, identifying the Word as bringing to birth the longing of the universe for the transfiguration of all things in the Spirit and in glory.

In the light of this creative vision we are forced to acknowledge the depth of our exile and the stifling nature of the time and space with which we have surrounded ourselves. Threatened by our fragility, we clasp and claim whatever might cloak the loneliness of our banishment. This human condition, however, is characterized not simply by our misdoing. At fault is our state of being—the very way we relate to each part of creation and to creation as a whole. The serpent was wise: "When you eat of it your eyes will be opened, and you will be like God" (Gen. 3:5). Neither Adam, nor Eve, nor we, seem able to resist the temptation of proprietorship—a desire that is the obsession dominating our space and threatening the future of every time.

5. The Human Condition

I remember a class I was teaching in theology. Near the end of the period, clearly in response to my lecture, a student asked: "Is it necessary for persons to be hurting

61

in order for them to find God?" The question forced me to be clear, first to myself. "Yes," I finally answered, "but not so we can find God. Awareness of our dislocation is necessary for God to find us." It always seems that a wound serves as opening for the Spirit, where God can be born within. It is when the soul is festering that the Spirit invades the center of our being, to *displace* us. And this rebirthing entails suffering at least as great as our mothers experienced at our first birth. Dorothee Soelle wisely discerned the dynamic informing almost all fairy tales: The lives of the "haves" are always placed in jeopardy.

All of us are exiles—resident aliens. We are damaged merchandise, every one. All of us are tainted by the sins of our parents, at least unto the third and fourth generations. Erik Erikson underscores how foundational it is for an infant to have a basic, original trust. Yet this needs to be in place soon after birth or one's sense of security is maimed. As we have seen, many children come into life without that basic trust, or if they have it early, soon gather sufficient reason to distrust. So deprived, from an early age we try somehow to earn the trust of others. In this condition of insecurity, Evelyn Underhill insists, we spend most of our lives conjugating three verbs: to want, to have, and to do. We crave, clutch, and fuss on all planes—the economic, political, social, emotional, and intellectual.

This condition and our futile efforts to assuage it squanders tendencies that could have provided us religious footings. Instead of experiencing *trust* as *tranquillity,* our state is that of perpetual anxiety, wrapped in unrest. In response, Underhill claims, we are tempted to diddle around with itsy-bitsy friends and meals and journeys for itsy-bitsy years on end. The monster created by Mary

Shelley's Dr. Frankenstein distills the dynamic behind these games we play. The monster was a gentle creature who desperately wanted friendship, but his appearance caused people to shun him. He came to be rejected, finally, even by his own creator. It was only then that he truly became a monster, as he internalized the rejection of those he had tried to befriend. And so it is with each of us: We are motivated by worry, and then deep fear, that we might be repulsive even to our own Creator.

Deep within us is a fear of being forgotten, coupled with the dread of being alone. As if this were not enough, such fear can become deadly when it becomes fixated with the sense of abandonment or having been discarded. In rigid response, we gather ingeniously around ourselves layers of pride, selfishness, greed, laziness, and hedonism. These, in turn, are rooted and well watered in the painful memories of prenatal and early scars.

Though we are born in the natural state of being like a timid yet wild animal, it is not long before we make the transition from "I can't" to "I won't." Every parent who has had a youngster will recognize this transition. Almost humorous, if they were not so lethal, are our absurd maneuvers of power, revenge, ambition, and the craving to dominate. I know of no church that does not have its share of persons who will not speak to other members, sometimes for years. Merton characterized such behavior as preferring to feed pigs than feast at the Father's table. What makes this personal state so difficult today is that we live in a society in which fragmentation occurs at most levels. Any resolution of this crisis depends on our ability to draw the crucial distinction between who we *think* we are and how deep is our *yearning*. We are forced to wander.

How many people have not yet been swallowed up entirely by a socially ascribed identity?

Over against this human condition, we are called to conjugate the verb *to be*. The goal is to be freed from our obsession with wanting, having, and doing. But since we are trapped in this downward spiral, any genuine transformation must come to us from outside ourselves. Or better yet, we need the *Outside* that is *within* us. Our hope at this point may be to discover within us traces of a silent reservoir of Mystery.

6. The Pilgrimage

The search for God today is rarely "successful," at least when approached directly. Whether one begins with the awareness that everything living is rooted in death, with everything serving as lunch for something else, or the massive presence of disease, or the societal thirst for violence, the path to God is obscure. There seems to be no map shepherding us from immersion in our chaotic world to being able to fall on one's knees in thankfulness. St. Teresa of Avila put it bluntly: "God, no wonder you have so few friends, the way you treat them." Dorothee Soelle made this dilemma structural, agreeing with Marx that religion is the sighing of an oppressed creation in the midst of a heartless world. Annie Dillard discerns her state as emerging at the intersection of two oceans, where beauty and horror meet, destined to be a hoax if the few moments of beauty are forgotten. One image that should burn into our souls is the motel ad carried by the Memphis newspaper one week before Martin Luther King, Jr., was assassinated at that very motel: "Vacation and relaxation without humiliation."

Not long ago the way that we theologians tried to reach society was through the human dilemma of experiencing profound guilt and craving a God who could touch our desperate need for forgiveness. We still experience this dilemma, for we certainly continue to wound and be wounded. There always seems to be someone before whom one's humility is challenged, one's patience taxed, or one's weakness made visible. Yet our reactions, once defined as "sin," are rooted in deeper causes—in garbled ambitions, failures, and hurts. Even depression is now clinically defined as resulting from wounded pride. The prayer for the daily office of Terce concludes, "If I am to be healed, it is you, Lord, who must heal me."

Yet in our society, these deeper causes are rarely broached, for even right and wrong have become so blurred that "sins" have been reduced to "mistakes," and remorse results only from being "caught." Guilt becomes a quaint pastime of the scandal newspapers at the grocery checkout. In fact, in our daily world, we think the wrong belongs not so much to guilty persons as to those who put "guilt trips" on others. There is hardly anything left that one could do and not be declared innocent if one has enough money to pay the right lawyer. Within such chaos, that which appears at all promising as a theological point of contact with society seems to be a recognition of God's involvement with us through variations on the theme of the *divine take-away*, in which God strips from us that which keeps us from God.

Particularly energetic today is the Holy Spirit who Francis Thompson's poem identifies as the "hound of heaven." Such a Spirit refuses to remain quiet, but steadily gnaws away at us, stripping away those promises by which our culture attempts to control us. For some of us the cracking occurs with these words: "Sorry, but you have cancer." Or after thirty-five years, one receives a pink slip from the corporation to which one has given a healthy share of one's life; with the pink slip comes the end of "security," even though one has played the societal game faithfully. A divorce, a suicide, an accident—any of these can serve as the particulars that crack the promises we once believed. But to rummage around the roots is to find something far deeper, as if woven into the fabric of existence itself. Grounding their insights in their own experiences, a number of spiritual writers today agree that God is best postulated from our *craving*. In identifying this condition, the most frequently used words are *hungering, thirsting, yearning, longing,* and *needing.* Freud was perceptive when he identified religion as residing in our endless wishing. Barth's diagnosis is even deeper: He insists that there is no inoculation for the incurable God-sickness. Likewise, Abhishikanda, the Benedictine monk who draws deeply from the spirituality of India, discerns that God is within the core of each of us, whom we experience in terms of call and longing. Sam Keen goes so far as to identify the human spirit as having been created to be consumed by longing, insatiability, and restlessness, necessitating a desire and longing for God. In the end, all these writers insist that to exist is to be in anguish, characterized by anxiety, loneliness, absurdity, discouragement, and the fear of failure, especially in the face of death.

Matthew Kelty is more pointed in perceiving our human condition as habituated by loneliness. Henri Nouwen, in turn, perceives loneliness as the modern sickness. We come into the world alone, no matter how many persons might be there. Our loneliness is infinite, a loneliness without measure. On this seashore one walks and ponders, says Kelty. Under this lonely sky one often stands, incapable of doing anything, for there is nothing one can do, but let it happen—let it sink in. The interiority in which God takes up residence is the size of the room of one's loneliness.

The writer of the book of Ecclesiastes not only agrees, but also hints that God creates our dilemma on purpose— having "put a sense of past and future into [our] minds, yet [we] cannot find out what God has done from the beginning to the end" (Eccles. 3:11). For some of us, the night is too long, and sooner or later, says Underhill, each of us will be assigned to the night shift. Yet to root this thirst for God either in our personal circumstances or even in the anatomy of our culture is to make its cause too peripheral to our existence. It is ontic, implanted in the very fact of existing. One either feels it, or one doesn't—but it is there. And if one does, Mystery is born. It resides in the awareness that without the Divine Presence, one simply would not be, in any and every sense of the word. God is essential for anything to be—then, now, always. In a real sense my life does not belong to me. It is given to me, moment by moment, as a gift that is renewable for a while. And I? I am a steward called to the task of bringing me into completion.

I remember some lines from a Broadway play whose name I cannot recall. The central actress needs to leave a Protestant worship service because of her laughter. "The Presbyterian God is too polite," she explained. "The only God I know is the one who quietly passes you by, or kicks in your back door after midnight." Simone Weil's analogy appears to echo these observations. To those who refuse to respond, God returns, again and again, like a beggar—until one day God just stops coming. And in the absence, clarity about one's origins renders life a pilgrimage for radical forgiveness.

God may paint the human condition on each of us with a fine portrait brush, but he gets our attention mostly when he paints with a broom. Much of Merton's appeal arises from the accuracy of his judgment on our times. We are in love with comfort, pleasure, material security, and trivial conversation about weather, the World Series, and the Super Bowl. Silence makes us nervous, he says, and prayer drives us crazy, with penance scaring us to death. Thus it is imperative for the Church to bring judgment against a society that judges everything according to what is saleable. What irony, that with two-thirds of the world starving, the goal in our country is to seek food that has no calories—as if the more worthless it is, the more it is sought. Soon, we will munch on strawberry-flavored cardboard, soaked in bottled water. In Kelty's eyes, our society is infantile in its need for something to drink, to chew, to suck, and to smoke. The image of life, American middle-class style, is existence in an enormous mall with no reason to leave. Behind it is a flea market for the lower class. And in the dumpsters behind both, the abandoned ones munch on breakfast. A child's verse for our times might well be "Humpty-Dumpty,"—the one about a downward fall, and the difficulty of putting things together again.

7. The Divine Craving

The attractiveness of monasticism in our day may be found in one sentence from the Prologue of St. Benedict's famous Rule: "Is there anyone here who longs for life and desires to see good days?"[6] Deep within each of us is a primal call to sacralize the time and space of our living, finding clues of meaning at their intersections. In seeking happiness, one is seeking God, although most likely unknowingly. But all such seeking fails to go very deep, until one becomes tired to death of running. With a shuddering of soul, and a stuttering of tongue, one senses that one is on the edge of an irreducible metaphysical hunger.

This pilgrimage of the heart is in truth an unquenchable groping toward Mystery. We can experience it as a desire seeking fulfillment, an emptiness yearning for fullness, and/or a trek moving toward sabbatical rest. Underhill sees it as the inevitability of a finite center of consciousness longing for Infinity. The unknown author of *The Cloud of Unknowing* calls it "longing Love," a waiting in the darkness—insatiable, restless, searching. Or again, a "dreadful hunger," involving "groaning and travailing in pain," with even the "answer" being an "absolutely ravishing experience." Others call it the universal craving to be whole. Taking a hint from the Eucharist, our spiritual journey is to sate a hunger and quench a thirst. And the name "God" is shorthand for that alone which can satisfy. Without God, the destiny of the human spirit is to be consumed by insatiable longing. Soelle's carefully chosen figures for our dilemma are fugitive, vagabond, and sojourner, seeking signs in the desert. She identifies the craving that matters as the need for something different, the wish to live differently, the need for a life that is not fragmented, the wish to be whole, and the passion to be free of calculation and fear.

At airports, as a moving escalator passes another going in the opposite direction, I often glimpse momentary snapshots of lonely persons in a hurry, lost in sad self-absorption. Such observations make some of us feel even more lonely, for so few people seem aware of humanity's absurd restlessness at the depth of our souls. Even so, such an awareness also makes clear the most incredible marvel that is happening in humanity. Out of the multi-millennial evolutionary carnage, *the* miracle is that the very *idea* of God should ever have arisen. Even to think of God, then, is to find oneself on the forward edge of time as evolution— even though the other travelers apparently have stepped off the escalator for an overpriced hot dog.

We are strange ones indeed, because if God does not exist, we are thunderstruck by the absurdness of the absence. As a professor, there were nights when I wondered if I was being immoral in cracking open the complacency of students by rendering them speechless before the "why" questions. Would they be better off in oblivion, than bitten by a Mystery that dooms them to be perennial searchers? Is it better to be certain about very little, but to crave much; or to crave a little and act as if one knows much? I concluded, for better or worse, that my task was to nip at their souls, and with Kierkegaard, to pour salt on open sores, and to wound from behind. I am not so much concerned about what "solution" they might find as I am that they know what Thoreau said so well: to live deliberately, and not discover when one dies, that one had not even lived. Soelle, too, is more concerned for the anatomy of the question than any particular "resolution." Whatever the "solution," it will inevitably involve a wager. And the deeper the question, the more profound will be the resolution implicit within the question. For the Christian, the healing paradox is this: *No one seriously seeks for God if God has not already found him or her.*

St. Bernard perceptively poses this divine-human intersection in different ways, until it sounds much like a divine riddle. God, no one can seek you who has not already found you. Or God, you seek to be found so that you may be sought for, sought so that you may be found. Or again, God, you seek us so that we will seek you, for you desire to be sought for, so that we may find you as the one who has already found us. The flavor of our craving is for our "beloved." And at its outermost edge, the search *for* God becomes a burning desire to be found totally *by* God.

The irony goes even deeper. The more one moves toward being an authentic self, the more one craves to give one's self away. The human search for fullness is in truth the passion to be lost in God. Once it is sensed deeply within, the yearning is present wherever one looks. At this moment outside my hermitage window, leaves flutter with the rich shades of autumn. Yet the shorter days hint of a sacred stillness soon to be, when one cold daybreak all will become lost in the winter time of Holy Waiting.

Although none of us likes to wait, there comes a moment when one finally knows that no created being, nor the possession of any thing, can fill the bottomless ache for which there is no medicine. There will come a further moment when one can finally confess that it is better to live with this ache than to be tempted by any of the available substitutes. Then, with this clarity comes a strange kind of breakthrough. One's passionate longing is no longer for that which is absent. Instead, *one's longing is the very nature of the divine-human love affair itself.* True birthing occurs through serious emptiness. Paralleling human love, the more one experiences moments with one's lover, the more intolerable separation becomes. Thus the ache itself is evidence of the authenticity of one's relationship with God, whose actual speaking is in silence.

As a child I could understand this, for no Christmas Day could ever match the mystery of anticipation called Christmas Eve. All of the major Christian festivals are woven in and out of Vigils—the prior evening in which one waits in foretaste. Especially significant are the mystery of Midnight Mass on Christmas Eve, and the rapture of Easter Vigil, which begins and ends in the speckled darkness of early morning. It is in anticipation, at the outer edge of our yearning, deeply in time, that Mystery births us.

8. Healing

In the end, that alone which will satisfy is not really that which will feed our hungry souls. What we need is that which can heal the hunger itself. In each of us this hunger is wrapped around root memories. Our search begins with the branches that are withering. From this one can move toward the main trunk that is losing bark. And finally, if we persist, we reach the rotting roots. It might sound simplistic to say that persons hurt others and themselves because they are starved for love and acceptance. And yet, ironic though it is, the deeper our underbelly of low self-esteem and vulnerability, the greater is our capacity for receiving grace. *The* spiritual need is finally to recognize that when viewed from God's perspective, we are of infinite value, loved unconditionally by the only One who matters. Reconciliation occurs when we recognize that if God is Love, then it is God who is the author of my longing and of my desire to love and be loved.

These moments of grace-filled healing can never remove the scars. And yet, that is part of the "miracle." Merton calls it being "scarred by joy." God can lead one to the point of forgiving those who have inflicted the bruises and scars. This is because, without them, I might never have recognized the finger touch of God. Soelle understands this well from her own hard experience. She identifies the hurtful persons in her life as symbols that receive life by being understood and accepted. But before such reconciliation is possible, we need our tottering survival mechanisms to dissolve. My relationship with my mother brought me to the "edge," yearning as I did for her unavailable affirmation. And yet, I look back now with amazement, because this negative situation forged in me a deep compassion for losers.

9. The Transfiguration of Motivation

Time as history comes into being when any part of the cosmos emerges into self-consciousness—that is, when it is capable of being conscious of itself. And yet it is this emergence which destines us to be exiles. Ants do what ants do, without pondering about options. And when a boot flattens their ant friends and blots out several months of their work, they do not speculate on the meaning of it all.

Those that remain just start building again. But when humans emerged from our animal base, both as a race and separately as individuals, self-consciousness brought a whole new state of being. With the ability to reflect on one's self, conscience is born, freedom becomes possible, and creativity is unleashed. But it also casts us out of Eden, for from that point on we become incapable of living without meaning. Thus freedom can become a burden, paralyzing us into indecision, or making us feel guilty for options not taken, and creativity becomes destructive as a competitive self-serving.

This condition contrasts heavily with the purity of heart that the Christian seeks. All depends on a transformation of one's *attitude* toward everything through one's *motive* being purified. There are three types of motivation. The first is *instrumental*, which means believing in order to receive something. "The family that prays together, stays together." Or some persons believe in order to escape hell. Others believe in the hope of being helped to become more successful salespersons. Others worship as respite from questionable business tactics. In fact, instrumental motivation characterizes the motivational level of much present-day evangelism. One is motivated to believe by the promise of reward, in this world or the next. But this kind of motivation is hardly different from the self-centered rewards our culture promises—the three P's of possessions, prestige, and power. The playing field may be different, but the motivation in both cases is self-serving.

The second type of motivation is *supplemental.* Here one's Church attendance functions on a par with other activities that supposedly mark a healthy, well-balanced person. The surprising rash of "family life centers" today, like bulging afterthoughts behind church buildings, illustrates a response to this motivation.

Quite different is *intrinsic* motivation. The most meaningful things in life are those valued for their own sake. Either one comes to experience this, or life as joy and beauty is simply unavailable. T.S. Eliot spoke of having the experience but missing the meaning. So it is here. Why sit for hours mesmerized by the ocean? What sense does that make? To see one wave is to have seen them all. Besides, who likes sand in their shoes? Or, what of the vee of birds flying south in the fall, to where I have never been? Feeling such ache is simply a painful distraction. Or what about the singing of a mockingbird, or a sonata by Mozart, or a spring rain, or coffee on a cold morning, or the giggle of a child, or the gaze of a lover? What good is any of this, other than wasting time that could better be used "productively"?

But to those whose life is centered intrinsically, one smiles deeply inside on hearing such questions. For the many who truly do not know what it means to be motivated intrinsically, all we can do is patiently play Bach's Suite No. 3 or lend them a novel by Fyodor Dostoyevsky. Again and again we can try, until the person hears "it" and sees "it"—or doesn't. All these experiences have a splendid value in being *intrinsic*: They are valuable for their own sakes, needing nothing more than themselves. So it is with God. However one may have begun one's relationship with the "Other," the pilgrimage remains insipid unless the relationship becomes intrinsic.

Using an analogy from daily friendships, no human relationship can survive if one person is continually asking for gifts. True friendship exists only when simply being together is more than enough. So it is with God. Truly to be in love with God is to want nothing more, for the relationship *itself* is its own reason for being. Here we can understand how the depth of faith can be measured by the deepness of our longing for God—for its own sake.

The story is told of three hermits who were permitted to visit a saintly man once each year. They would come to his hermitage in the desert, and two of the men would ask questions of the saint. The third man kept silent. After many years, the saintly man finally asked the silent hermit: "Don't you have any questions to ask that might make your visit of value?" "No. It is enough simply to be with you."

To live intrinsically is to experience the sacred nature of time and space, for its own sake. We can depict such meaning in several ways: as the sacralizing of the world, or the pilgrimage into God, or the Kingdom as the consummation of history. All of these expressions point to the Mystery known intrinsically as foretaste. For those who see, nothing more is needed or wanted. In fact, the capacity to see in this fashion is itself a gift, made possible because the Spirit has touched our eyes, anointed our ears, cleansed our tongues, massaged our fingers, and opened wide our nostrils. For those who know in this way, one wants nothing more than "to grow old loving one's God"—perhaps with Mozart and ice cream on Sundays. Either one sees it, or one doesn't.

With this transformation of motivation comes also a new way of speaking. The language is that of the "nuptial chamber" and is distinct from the everyday language of commercial transaction. Learning to speak as a lover and poet is fundamental for those who would believe. "Two times two" dare not always be four. In fact, today's sterility is rooted in the binary, with everything either on or off, yes or no, up or down—until our eyes glaze over and our ears become deaf. The soul dies without the "maybes," the "almosts," and the "what ifs." Poets dance among imagery and similes and analogies. Their hope is to be grasped by an image that might evoke the meaning of the whole. But images can be likely candidates only if they include the daisies dancing by the wayside, a deer soaring over a fence, and tall trees embracing azure skies. We are never certain about very much, until we experience these unique moments within special time. Then the unclear takes on the aura of Mystery, and we can live more gracefully with the questions.

Conversion is evident when, gifted with lover's eyes, the contemporary world of power, prestige, and possessions seems quite silly. In becoming gloriously alive, one is grasped by the *preciousness of living*. Experiencing intrinsically, then, the Christian tenaciously becomes involved in social justice. We have little option but to oppose those who violate life's preciousness and to side especially with those who are discarded or violated. Karl Barth understands this connection by insisting that to clasp one's hands in prayer is to begin an uprising against the world's disorder. William Law's response is also apt: that the Christian is called not to be uncommonly good, but heroically faithful. And Fr. Joseph Braddock makes an important observation for those involved in parish ministry: Being at the altar doesn't validate our social ministry. Rather, what we do out in the world validates what we do at the altar.

10. The Church and Formation

To declare that there is no salvation outside the Church need not be heard as arrogant proprietorship. At its best, the statement acknowledges that Christian existence entails a lengthy formation. In fact, one is always *becoming* a Christian, for the transformation involved is no less than turning things upside down. This the individual cannot accomplish alone. We are trapped within a societal and personal maze, as well as by our human condition. Even if one wants conversion, the only motivation we could have for wanting it is rooted in the self's own self-serving. Thus everything we do is inevitably desecrated by selfishness. Merton acknowledges this entrapment by identifying the *imago Dei* as the capacity to give one's self away. This is precisely what the self-serving self cannot do. Therefore if conversion does occur, it witnesses to the presence of grace.

Teilhard de Chardin wisely characterizes this conversion. There is a point in one's pilgrimage when the soul knows that it has taken its fill of the universe and of the self. From that point on, the soul is possessed by an indescribable need to die to self and to leave behind all vestiges of that self. This conversion of motivation is possible only through an ongoing transformation that requires *a deep and lengthy process of formation.* Here we can understand the place of the Church. Whether this formation comes before or after the conversion, to be "born again" entails ongoing discipline in an intentionally Christian context. What is more, this community needs to be clearly counter-cultural, for above all one must lose one's very taste for the "rewards" of modern culture. A clue that the transformation is becoming deep is when one finds humorous the desire to *want* to win the lottery—or even a pink Cadillac. Merton's hope is that the "monk" in each of us will whisper to us its sneaky hunch that the claims of the world are fraudulent. Always aware that we are just on this side of death's edge, we are brought to the essence of Christian existence: that the meaning of one's life rests on divine promises. So the psalmist says: "If you uphold me by your promise I shall live; let my hopes not be in vain" (Ps. 119:116 GRAIL). To wager on promise is to live in Mystery.

At this point, we can see the trap of believing that only the uncommitted are free, or even that one can live without making significant decisions. What makes Christians different is our *choice* of the time and space in which our formation shall take place. William James knew that formation begins with the intent to act one's self into a particular way of being. Similar is Wesley's advice to a doubting preacher: that he should preach the gospel until he believes it. Christianity is a special way of seeing and hearing, requiring a wager before it can occur. What happens after that is a personal and corporate work of imagination.

An example is the imaginative power and genuine joy of the rare child at play, one who has not yet been seduced by toys of plastic noninvolvement. Such toys do not invite imagination at all, for dolls talk for themselves, and hobbies are reduced to pushing plastic "tab A" into a less-than-obvious "slot B." "Unless you change and become like children, you will never enter the kingdom of heaven" (Matt. 18:3). Faith is the imaginative stance by which the primal image is permitted to flood time and space with play. The child immersed in imagination is a powerful image for the Christian. Faith begins with a story, the story of God's incarnation in the event called Jesus Christ. All else, especially in the Triduum, is an imaginative acting out of the sacredness involved within that premise. We worship what we love, and love what we worship.

Another analogy that might be helpful here is learning to love classical music. It is a process of listening until one hears beneath the notes. For those who listen but cannot yet hear, one may select carefully the composer and composition for them, but one can do little more. One hears or one doesn't, and when one does, we gladly acknowledge it is a "gift." So it is for the Christian. Our whole vocation in this life involves a special stance, one that is most likely to occur through immersion in the sacralized time and space of the Church's life. Pentecost is the birthday of the Church, for then it was that the Holy Spirit made the Church a divine-human reality. The Church became a living organism, one that for us involves a way of being, a style of becoming, a manner of seeing, a love of hearing, and a way of gambling. The price for admission is the clarity of knowing that there is no escaping from the yearning deep within. I sought thee where thou was not, said Augustine, for I sought thee not within myself.

Judgment falls heavily upon the Christian churches at this point. For Christian formation to be authentic, it must dilute our appetite for what modern society offers as a lure. But to restore the Church's capacity for evoking change this deep, even our analogies require conversion. The present fad is to model the Church in terms of business processes and language. The Church is pictured as being a business, with a bureaucracy intent on fulfilling efficiently the desires of their "customers." But that imagery is all wrong. Not only is the Church not a business; at its heart it is not even an institution. Our urgent need is to rediscover images capable of reclaiming the essential nature of the Church as *organic*. The Church is deeply *alive*, an organism, with each of us vital participants in every part, from heart to fingernails. Renewal requires nothing less that discovering in a deeply mysterious way that the Church is the very "Body of Christ," with Christ organically the head.

Unfortunately, we are engulfed by the efficient machines and fabricated products of our ever more rapid technology, and we become impatient with the slow organic processes of growth. Yet against modern society, the Church must stand straight and true in her calling. She is no less than "Holy Mother Church," alive with the rich Mysteries that intersect spacious time and timeless space. The transcendent dimension of the Church is Jesus Christ in ongoing Incarnation.

11. A Postmodern Context

Ours is the age called "postmodern." Its dual inceptions were Auschwitz and Hiroshima. In these events we experienced full-blown the "terror of history" and the "horror of place"—the time and space of our cultural life. Such imagery at the edge of the millennium presses heavy upon us. Perhaps at no other time have we felt so much the massive power of a complex and convoluted world that is deeply out of control. Those called "leaders" govern by polls, dependent for campaign funds on the monopolies that in turn control markets and legislatures. No one is managing the whole, which instead is madly ruled by self-interest.

Our culture, which is so intent on having the "latest" of everything, is at the same time enamored by a nostalgia for the 1950s—in dress, architecture, furnishings, even greeting cards. The fifties were the sentimental period before the societal upheaval of the sixties. Such an obsession with the past may suggest that we are in exile from even our own frightening present. Our hope lies in the number of persons who are feeling the fault lines beneath our plastic comfort and are pursuing the search for spiritual integrity while "London Bridge is falling down." Emerging is a call for the Church to become countercultural, to offer an alternative, organic way of life.

12. Vision and Pure Faith

As a graduate philosophy student at Yale, I took some courses in theology. After one year, I hit an impasse. I came to the conclusion that without the resurrection of Jesus there would be no Christianity and thus no Church. Since I did not believe that dead people get up and walk around after three days, my flirtation with Christianity was over. Yet soon after that, I awoke to a morning, beautiful to the extreme. I discovered, strangely, that the question on my mind was no longer "Did Jesus rise from the dead?" Rather, I was claimed by a new question: "What difference would it make if he did?" My studies began to focus on this question. I finally found the clue for which I was searching in the final chapter of the book of Revelation. There it was, the fullness for which I had been unconsciously craving for a lifetime. It touched profoundly my childhood, born in Appalachia to a coal miner's family along a sulfur creek—a family always behind financially, scrambling just "to make it." Every relative I had was either dead from the mines or maimed in some way.

It was with such Appalachian eyes and ears that I read: "Then I saw a new heaven and a new earth . . .prepared as a bride adorned for her husband. . . . See, the home of God is among mortals . . . . He will wipe away every tear from their eyes. Death will be no more; mourning and crying and pain will be no more, for the first things have passed away" (Rev. 21:1-4). Here was promised a time and a space where none of our struggles or pains or confusions or hopes or even death shall ever be lost—for they are taken into God. This is what is at stake for the Christian if Christ rose from the dead. Here, at its best, we have the imagination of the remembering community.

I knew what I had now. *I had a vision, fit for a life's wager.* I could drink to the "dream." And my wager was this: If there is a God who makes this divine-human promise, we will be co-creators. But if the vision is only a cruel tease, I will still live the vision so that my life is a protest against a Godless universe. Kathleen Norris made a helpful observation here. To appreciate the relevance of the virgin martyrs for our own time, she said, we need not ask whether the saint "really" existed, but rather, why it would have been necessary to invent her. Carl Braaten adds a further thought: that a person cannot say "no" unless she or he has captured an alternative with the imagination.

I find fascinating the final time of the young Therese of Lisieux. After years of sensing God's intimate presence, she lost it all. But, ironically, it was in this "absence" that her mature spiritual breakthrough came. She recognized that it was God who permitted her to be overwhelmed by impenetrable darkness. Hers was not an exception. For many Christian saints, *"pure faith"* emerges only when, as in Psalm 88:19 (GRAIL), one comes to the place where "my one companion is darkness." Pure faith, heroic faith, is to experience the cold breath of Nothingness, and *still hold steadfast to the dream.* So understood, vision becomes a practiced Mystery. The wager needed is believing in God's presence without trying either to understand it or even to feel it. In fact, if one needs either understanding or feeling in order to believe in God, then God would no longer be a matter of faith—of *trusting the divine promises.*

Teresa of Avila is very clear about this. After years without a direct experience of God, she entered a period of intense raptures. Even then, she insisted, such experiences are not a sufficient basis for a conclusion about God. These special feelings may come into one's state of faith. If so, our response is to give thanks to God for the undeserved gift. But *never* should they be used as scaffolding to hold the vision. Jesus' response to Thomas is central to this point: "Have you believed because you have seen me? Blessed are those who have not seen and yet have come to believe" (John 20:29). To trust the promises is all we have. It is sufficient.

How beautiful is the musical resolution after a seventh chord. That for which we as Christians yearn is that somewhere, sometime, the seventh chord of all time will be resolved in beauty. As the beginning of a seminar lecture, I went to a piano and played a scale, but left off the final note. There was a murmuring in the room, until one courageous

84

person ran to the piano and sounded the missing note. So is the Christian's approach to time.

13. God

In a profound sense, God is the only subject worth pondering. As some persons are beginning to do just that, an awareness is emerging that in our society *more* is *less*. The search focuses on a Mystery in which one can lose one's self, and in that loss to be full. And a number of these persons seem willing to risk believing that "to long for" is to be "longed by," that to lose is to find, to be haunted implies a "by whom," and to yearn for a Love still unknown is truly to be loved.

Soelle identifies Christian faith as the attempt to drive back the boundaries of the absurd. But such an effort itself seems to be absurd. The more we ponder, the more we seem driven to acknowledge that it is impossible, based on the world's condition, to move toward belief in a God. And yet, with a mood of gentle trust, we can also acknowledge that it is just as impossible to doubt that, at the root of all things, there is a profound Silence. Each day we walk the knife-edge of that Mystery—between the unlivable encounter with Nothingness and the invasive mystery at the depth of our souls.

On the one hand, no one would choose to fall into the hands of the God of Scripture. And yet, deep within, where the "still small voice" has apparently taken up residency, a strange assurance haunts us that our greatest chance at perfection is our need for such a God. At times it may be enough to trust the Mystery—and let our insanity be that of loving in a loveless world and forgiving in an unforgiving society.

14. The Search for a Primal Image

When we grapple with understanding anything of importance, we speak with analogies, distilled as images. It follows, then, that the uppermost goal of one's pilgrimage is to be discovered by a *primary* image, so powerful that it is able to hold in place most of the assorted pieces of one's life. Such an image gives birth to a basic rhythm and liturgy. Put another way, our existential task is to discover a primal image sufficient to sacralize our time and space. Underhill insists that such a primal image must be able to stand in the face of two gnawing voices—that of death and that of our animal nature.

Merton was the master of images, and yet he was never able to come up with *the* image. This accounts, at least in part, for an ambiguity not only within his writing, but also in his life. He seemed to waiver among three images, any one of which could be a viable candidate:

1. God drawing the world back into God's own Self.
2. The Primal Desire of loving God and being loved.
3. Experiencing the radical contingency of every-thing that exists, and thus exposing the necessity of God as the Ground of one's existence.

At the end of his life, famed scientist Sir Arthur Eddington shared a primal image as the conclusion of his life's work: "Something Unknown is doing we don't know what." Yet in his earlier yearnings, some dim contours of this "Unknown" had begun to show. One of his most suggestive images was that the more he probed into the primal nature of energy, the more did it resemble Mind. The primal images of other thinkers emerge in spatial terms: that there are places where we can place the soles of our feet on the soul of the world. Still other thinkers find their primal image as a Mystery in which the inner vibrations of atoms and living cells are unified with the enigmatic dance of slow-turning galaxies. Other thinkers ponder *time* as their referent, speaking, for example, of the times of intersection in which we "hear" the heartbeat of the universe in the Mystery of pure Silence. The poet in each of us knows beyond knowing that blessed are the homesick for they shall come home. Blessed is the courage of the long distance runner. And blessed are the lovers who meet their rendezvous.

Our concern in sacralizing time and space, then, is to discern an image by which to heal the broken dreams of the world. In sharing these images with our fellow searchers we may gain a taste for what we have almost lost: the meaning of Christian existence. Living as a Christian means living "as if," testing our diverse images and sharing our stories with fellow travelers in the hope of being seized by one image that implies them all.

CHAPTER FOUR

Theologically Based Experience

"You have appointed the bounds that [we] cannot pass." (Job 14:5)
"O Lord, you have searched me and known me." (Ps. 139:1)
"On that day you will have no other questions to ask me." (John 16:23)

1. The Emergence of Doctrine

We have suggested that the natural growth process can meaningfully be understood as pilgrimage. In turn, we have drawn the connection between the needs that inform the human pilgrimage and the Mystery of the Church. A growing life before birth is particularly sensitive to its surroundings. In the early postbirth years, the child develops life-characteristics that further provide the rhythms of his or her life for years to come. By understanding how fundamental for a person's growth are the early contours of one's time and space, the Church has the vital responsibility to keep rediscovering and offering a profoundly Christian environment.

We can offer such an environment in two related ways. First, we must sense and develop the deep connections between the normal hinge events of the human pilgrimage and the Church's Sacraments and sacramental acts issuing from the Mystery that is the Church. Second, we need to explore the relationship between "secular" time and the Church's transformation of time in liturgy. Kathleen

Norris in *The Cloister Walk* calls liturgy a metaphorical exchange, giving rise to theology. Expressed another way, liturgy is poetry, and theology is prose. Learning to speak the language of faith in both forms is crucial for attaining a deep faith. Finally, by exploring the sacredness of time, space, and their intersections, we can discover how fundamentally different is the life of the Christian from the way in which others live and domesticate their lives.

Those in the early Church searched their own lives and Hebraic history for analogies that could provide a formative environment akin to that from which Jesus and his initial disciples emerged. Certain images emerged that grasped and evoked the nature and meaning of faithful living better than others did. We have indicated that it was Israel's exile to Babylon that evoked the need to gather together writings in order to preserve the people's identity. This resulted in what we call the Old Testament, the writings by which Jews refused to forget who they were. Likewise, it was in a time of persecution that the early Christians felt the need to focus the lives of the faithful, making clear what was not negotiable, even in times of torture and martyrdom.

This focusing process had two dimensions. First was the need to "translate" from their own experiences the deepest analogies by which they could retain and share the lived meaning of the "good news." This involved a reciprocity with the second dimension, which was "liturgy." Liturgy became a way of celebrating and bringing alive this new, emerging Christian way of life. Liturgy, meaning the "work of the people," is a living process of distilling the imagery of faithfulness. This, in turn, emerges through acts of doing, believing, and sharing—privately, corporately, and publicly as evangelism. Through this process of faithful living, certain vigorous analogies attained a "thickness," and their frequent observance became a priority because of their emotional power.

This mutual process of discernment, through a natural and inevitable distilling, established conceptual summaries called "doctrines." All pilgrimages are processes that establish precedent and priority. Experience births images; imagery births increasingly inclusive analogies. These, in turn, are rehearsed as liturgy. Liturgy, in turn, gives rise to conceptual theology. And this theologizing, in time, distills its foci into doctrines. So the circle goes, on and on—in the Church as a whole, and within each of us, in a community of supportive accountability.

2. The Universal Questions

To understand the ability of the Christian faith to sacralize time and space, we need to understand that the Church's "doctrines" do not stand on their own. In fact, taken by themselves, they make little sense. It is crucial that we see why. Doctrines are attempted "answers" to unavoidable "questions." The relevance of these answers, in turn, depends on the purity and universality with which the questions themselves are posed. These, in turn, continue to be tested as to the degree to which the lived answers form a particular "world" that gives vital shape to one's time and space. Episcopal Bishop John Shelby Spong rightly says that truth is not to be found in the doctrines themselves, but in the experience to which each doctrine points. Even though coming from a contrasting theological perspective,

THEOLOGICALLY BASED EXPERIENCE

Donald Bloesch in his *Evangelical Theology* agrees with Spong, acknowledging that theology is at its best when emerging from "the thoughtful tendrils of image and feeling." And shouting, adds J.A.T. Robinson, is the medium of proclamation.

The questions from which doctrines follow are themselves universal, while the answers are contingent. This contingency depends on how a particular community poses and understands the questions, and how well the answers are lived. Within the Christian Church, it took several centuries for this doctrinal process to be set in place, virtually the time it took the Church to develop from a *movement* to its emergence as an *institution.* Joseph Martos calls this the gradual movement from metaphorical description to metaphysics.

As we move toward understanding how the meaning of the Christian faith finds its center in the sacralizing of time and space, we need to recognize how the major Christian doctrines emerged from the unavoidable questions posed by life itself.

DOCTRINE:	QUESTION:
Human Nature	"Who were we meant to be?
Human Condition	"Who are we now?"
Fall	"How can we account for the gap between nature and condition?"
Sin	"What is wrong, for which we are responsible?"
Evil	"What went wrong, for which we are not responsible?"
Christology	"Who can change this situation?" (Who is the "Christ"?)

Atonement	"How can the situation be changed?"
Justification	"When does this change happen?"
Sanctification	"To what effect does this change occur?"
Church	"Where does this change happen?"
Kingdom	"For what goal does this change happen?"
God	"In Whom or What is this process grounded?"

How these questions are formed, and how liturgy leads to the emergence of doctrines as answers, are anything but rational processes, at least in their inception. Early religion was "danced" before it was "believed." Music has always been involved in religion, from its inception to its most complex expressions. To chant the psalms is to pray twice. While Gordon D. Kaufman sees this process as one of "imaginative construction," this is too self-conscious. Long before such conscious expressions appear is a functional distillation, an ongoing discernment that correlates with a community's deepest needs and is expressed best with a poet's eye and a lover's ear.

The process, then, is this: Christian doctrines emerge through the ongoing engagement with "universal" questions, lived as answers in a particular place of time and space in the Church's history and location. As one might expect, this parallels in intriguing fashion what occurs within each of our own personal pilgrimages. In one sense, the canon differs for each person, because the flavor of the questions as lived depends on the particularities each person experiences. The questions we identified emerge out of a person's pilgrimage, and, at the same time, they give shape to that pilgrimage.

3. Walking into One's Weakness

Often I am asked to speak on the subject of "Finding God in Today's World." The introduction to my lecture is usually designed to say straight out, "We cannot find God. God finds us. All we can do is put ourselves in God's way." Put another way, we fall into God's embrace by walking down the corridor of our weakness. For the extrovert, I recommend the profound silence of a Quaker meeting. For the introvert, try the amazing energy of a storefront charismatic service. For the perennially talky Protestant, try a Roman Catholic Church at sunset, alive with the mystery of candles, incense, and color. For the Catholic, I recommend a Protestant sermon, carefully articulated so as to challenge one to become faithfully articulate. For me, an energetic extrovert, my "mistake" was my curiosity. It led me to a Trappist monastery, set in a valley around which mountains serve as sentinels. I was bitten, first by the mystery of silence. Then what claimed me was the Eucharistic gesture, lifting toward the mountains the chalice holding the whole of creation, to be returned blessed. Bathed in silence, I was claimed by the rhythm that touched the furthest stars and the little frog that kept looking for me.

Based on my experience, I believe conversion occurs when we are claimed by an intersection of time and space that we experience as sacred. On the mountaintop with his sheep, Moses was told to remove his shoes, for he stood on holy ground. For me, I was on horseback, herding the monastic cattle. I remember dismounting. I remember hugging the horse. I remember both of us waving at the peaks. This was a sacred intersection of time with space, where at least for a moment, everything made sense. I knew that I would be different, and there wasn't much I could or wanted to do about it. This is the way I described the implications in my journal:

> These monks are subversives. In a culture of noise, these little white-robed monks who like to play with bells choose silence; in a culture of work, they choose contemplation; in a culture of self-realization, they renounce the self; in a culture of achievement, they declare that the winner will be loser and only the loser winner; in a culture whose economy is utterly dependent on consumption, they insist on emptiness; in a culture structured by possession, they insist upon detachment; in a culture of complexity, they call us to the simplicity of willing one thing; in a culture intent on a high standard of living, they insist on a high standard of life. Achievement versus grace; the exposure of the emptiness of fullness for the fullness of emptiness. The heart of this subversion is in planting within a person the appetite for silence. And once planted, once one tastes silence, and listening, and stopping, and being flooded by a Depth beyond all words, once one lets go so that one's hands are empty for perhaps the first time, once you do nothing, say nothing, think nothing, but just let yourself *be* in the sacred mist of a morning valley, or the eyes of a child at play, if you ever let this happen, it is all over for you. From then on, everything else seems insane.

How weird my pilgrimage became from that point. Although the father of five, I live now as a hermit in the

Ozark Hills. From a chaplain in the 1960s for the Black Panthers, I am now a monk living in a county so poor that the liquor store went bankrupt. Strange indeed, that after thirty-five years of professional talking as a professor, I should have been so claimed by the Silence of God that I took early retirement. And after forty years as an ordained United Methodist, I recently became a Roman Catholic priest. To those who kept asking me "why?", my answer seems so simple now. I didn't know it very well at the time, but I know now that the primal image that had bitten me is the Eucharist as the distillation of the Mystery of existence. It meant lifting up daily the paten of pain and yearning and brokenness of the world, lifting everything into God's own becoming, forever. It is to drink the cup of joy with friend or stranger, intoxicated by the sheer delight of simply being alive. It has resulted in my seeing the ordinary as extraordinary. It means seeking the sacredness in all time and space, and letting my small life inch back a little the drifting sands of my own society. God is the name I give to the intense feeling of such strangeness—a leading that is not of my doing.

4. The Awakening

Perhaps the culprit is Thoreau, or at least he understood. As we mentioned, he gave this reason for going to his own hermitage on Walden Pond: "I wished to live deliberately, to front only the essential facts of life, and see if I could not learn what it had to teach, and not, when I came to die, to discover that I had not lived. I did not wish to live what was not life; living is so dear."[1] He and I seem to have been found by the same God, through a process I call "negative grace." Positive grace refers to God's graciousness in "showering gifts on his beloved." "Negative grace," although still emerging from God's graciousness, is experienced as a game of "take-away," in which God strips us, removing things that are barriers to a naked confrontation. God takes away distraction after distraction, until our time and space take on the harsh contours of the desert.

For many of us, negative grace has to do with the erosion and disintegration, and even betrayal, of the American dream. How startling it is to be told by professional medical surveys that at least 70 percent of sickness sufficient to warrant treatment is really "psychosomatic." This does not mean that it is made-up. It means that the cause is a sickness of soul. Jung agreed, claiming that most of the clients who came to him were bitten deeply by religious questions. Menninger, in turn, identified that what a great number of mental patients really yearn for is to hear words of absolution for their sins.

"Spirituality" is the name for this strange yet inevitable pilgrimage on which each of us has embarked. We could call it "lived theology," with theology being "articulated spirituality," rendered self-conscious. Or again, spirituality emerges from living deeply the questions. No one has any option but to decide answers to the questions or to act in such a way that answers are assumed. The working assumption of "keeping on keeping on" is that it is better to live than to die. Either this is so, or die we will, trying to stifle the questions, one way or another. For many, their spirituality is not self-conscious. Daily we live the "plot" of our pilgrimage, yet we feel depressed either because we do not know what the plot is or doubt that there is one.

Few of us know who we are really. Our life is like reading a novel, yet finding no clues as to what the plot is really about.

I remember only too well my doctoral graduation. As my roommate and I went down the steps from the platform, he mumbled to me: "This diploma tells the world that I know what almost all the important religious figures believe, but I'll be damned if I know what I believe about hardly anything." Within several years the truth of his statement had led me to a different way of teaching doctrine, far different from how I had been taught. I began with Augustine, who discerned that we have no option but to love. Thus what determines everything we do is who or what is the object of our "supreme love" (*ordo amoris*). Luther was likewise helpful in insisting on the distinction between *assensus* (belief) and *fiducia* (trust). One can believe that Australia is an island, but that has little significance for how I live my life. What makes all the difference is that upon which I *trust* my life.

Spirituality, then, has more to do with faithfulness than with having faith. Tillich used the language of "ultimate concern." Of all animals, we alone can (and must) ask the question "Why?" And we alone have an ultimate concern as our answer, which we cannot live without assuming. For example, picture Elsie, Borden's "contented cow." Suppose I interrupt Elsie's contented mooing among the daisies with this news: "Do you know *why* they have given you this whole meadow? So as to fatten you. And do you know why? Because they are going to eat you this fall!" And how does Elsie respond to this news? "Moo," she responds contentedly.

In contrast, our uniqueness and our downfall is that in being human, we can understand only too well what Elsie is utterly incapable of grasping. We are going to die, each of us, and all that separates us from six feet deep—or from the undertaker's rosebed—is time. The issue is not "whether" but "when." And on this edge emerges the incredible Mystery of choosing life in the face of death's inevitability. This is spirituality. Lived corporately, it is liturgy; rendered self-conscious, it is theology; and codified into systematic answers, it is Christian doctrine. It is in this sense that just as the Church is the soul of the world, so is liturgy the soul of the Church.

5. The Impossibility of Atheism

Such thinking brings us to a crucial conclusion. Each person has a "functional" God, maybe more than one, in the sense that "god" is the name for one's center of gravity. Thus in a significant sense, the question "Is there a God?" is irrelevant. Functionally, there are no real atheists. There are only those whose pilgrimage has not yet pushed them to the rim of conscious awareness of the working meaning they have unknowingly assumed. The issue is not *if*, but *who* or *what*. Stated biblically, wherever our "treasure" is, there is our soul (Luke 12:34). Diagrams 1 and 2 illustrate the central issue at stake.

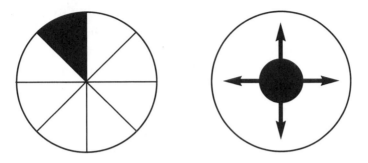

The first diagram indicates with the darkened slice *the place of theology* in most seminaries. It is a subject matter to be mastered, along with subjects like preaching, Church history, and the Bible. The second diagram illustrates how "lived theology" or "spirituality" needs to stand at the center of one's living, providing the "why" as one's orientation to all other subjects. To teach theology in this sense begins with helping the student render self-conscious this theological working assumption that the student already has. Not only does this exercise give thickness to the working assumption by exploring the doctrinal answers that follow, but it also helps to bring coherence to the time and space of one's life.

The first diagram can also illustrate the false way in which many Christians understand the *place of the Church* in one's life. Here the church takes its place among other acceptable institutions for living a "full" and "prosperous" life. The second diagram, however, illustrates the real place of the Church for Christians, where one's life is formed and sustained. Either it is the central activity and claim of one's life, or one's claim to be Christian is spurious.

These two illustrations also provide the same contrast when applied to *one's personal life*. In the first diagram the Christian faith assumes one slice of a person's allegiance, along with other dimensions such as one's political party, one's job, the Rotary, the local country club—and Monday Night Football. The second diagram illustrates the meaning of "faith" as the functional center from which one's motives, actions, and the momentum for one's memberships flow.

The Church must reclaim its mission to create and live within its sacralized time and space. The present hope is that a number of Christians are making this rediscovery. Genuine evangelism happens when persons are invited into the special world of a local church, where through liturgy one is grasped by what it is like to live self-consciously from its radiant center.

6. Faith and Self-Deception

The irony of faith is that one's functional "ultimate concern" is largely *unknown, unrecognized,* and *unconscious.* Thus spiritual growth depends on bringing into consciousness one's "functional god." "Freudian slips" and dreams are both helpful as hints, but spiritual direction is crucial if this discernment is to be honest. One needs someone, or a group, that will guide one to see beneath and behind one's surface appearances. Jesus said that by their fruits you will know them, and so it is with every possession one has. In fact, one's identity is emitted by one's favorite color, pictures on the wall, one's preferred chair, the placement of the desk in one's office, and one's favorite music. One's library also holds good evidence of who a person is, or when, as it were, one died.

A major calling for the Church, then, is to help persons discern the real plot they are living and support them with a love that enables them to face steadily the mirror of self-disclosure. Looking in this mirror, they may be claimed by joy, for who they are is who they have wanted to be. In that case, we proclaim, "Alleluia!" On the other hand, one's most appropriate response may be to vomit in disbelief at how one has lived—but then one is ripe for conversion. Either way, a huge responsibility of the Church is to provide a means of accountability whereby each parishioner may be faithfully disciplined.

As an aide in helping persons discover themselves through one-on-one spiritual direction, I developed a "Sentence Completion Exercise" and an "Image Association Inventory." [See Appendices 4 and 5.] Both are ways of tricking the unconscious into releasing some of its secrets. One can create such an instrument by writing a series of partial sentences such as these: "What I most regret doing is _____," or "Parents should _____." These exercises I find more helpful than most of the professional tools I use.

Another simple method is to prepare a series of questions, such as those in Appendix 1. I have used these frequently in groups, asking the questions out loud at a speed that forces people to write their answers quickly. Then we number off for sharing in pairs. When the group reconvenes after an hour, I have yet to find any response other than that the experience was highly helpful. And while most of the participants had previously said they did not know how to find a "spiritual director," in almost every case the pairs created at random indicated that they could easily see themselves being "spiritual directors" for each other.

As a way of illustrating the diverse pilgrimages of different persons, I spent an evening carefully choosing nine pieces of contrasting music. After I finished playing these pieces of music in class, a student leveled me with the comment: "While the form is different, professor, each of those pieces is a variation on the 'blues.'" He was right. I should have known, because each piece I chose was a favorite of mine. In another class, I spoke about theologizing from the environment in which one lives. During the break, several students went to my office and theologized about what they saw. The report they gave to the class was on the mark.

When I attended seminary, a required course was Theology 101, taught from the perspective of primary Christian doctrines. It wasn't until much later that I became aware that the class was based on a misleading assumption: that I was not a "theologian" until Niebuhr taught me to be one. But what this course actually taught me was how Niebuhr did theology, even while he attempted to keep private his own "spirituality" on which it was really based. What was totally neglected, or probably unknown, was any acknowledgment that the "theologizing process" for each student had already begun months before we were born. Further, doctrine was taught as a "given," as though understandable in isolation. The class neglected the fundamental questions out of which Christian doctrines have been proposed as answers. It is amazing how many games are rooted in the attempt to "reach home." We should have been taught that this is so with theology, too. It was only much later through spiritual direction that I finally understood the fourfold theological task best identified as spirituality: *support, discernment, options, discipline.*

7. The Necessity of Spiritual Direction

Religion at its best is *the total response of the entire person to the whole of life.* "Spiritual direction" is a primary vehicle in enabling this response to happen, mirroring back the life of those who ask to see who they hunger to be. A "spiritual director" is one who knows you so well that she or he can sing your song when you are on the verge of forgetting the words. This process is fundamental for the Christian, representing on the personal plane a primary reason for the Church's existence. While spiritual direction may sometimes be nondirective, at other times the director asks probing questions. The task is like being a midwife, whereby through pain there is birth and rebirth. The way to verify if one's "God," inhabiting one's time and space, is really "true," is through "livability," in self-conscious and disciplined living, "as if" it is true. In volume one of his *Systematic Theology,* Paul Tillich states well the principle. One must discern if one's "God" can be trusted without betrayal and obeyed without idolatry. I perceive that the widespread interest in spirituality today is because our societal gods are failing. Such failing can infect one's marriage, one's children, one's job, one's health, one's security. The current trio that are causing people to radically question their lives are downsizing, cancer, and divorce. What then? Or where then? Or even more basic, why?

8. Theology as Autobiography

All theology, in the end, is autobiographical. Early on, one's life seems characterized by options and choices for one who is, presumably, in control. But as life goes on, one can recognize that one has less control than one originally thought. Obstacles pop up like prairie dogs, as one's goal becomes increasingly unclear. The older we become, the shorter and faster time is, and increasingly we can see the blemishes caused in our space by use and by neglect. We become like Pirandello's play *Six Characters in Search of an Author.* Our craving increasingly is to believe that there really is a plot to our life. The most ominous shadow is that we will reach the "end," whatever that might mean, only to find that our pilgrimage has been like a tale told by an idiot, full of sound and fury, signifying nothing. Plot is what gives form to the whole, rendering it a pilgrimage. This plot, in turn, is centered in a primal image. And this primal image is what provides the pattern for the whole of one's life.

Listening to stories is a favorite activity for young children. Interestingly, the older one gets, the more stories regain exceptional appeal. And just as the child always has a favorite story, so the older adult seems led to rummage through the clutter to discover a Story of stories. It needs to be a story whose plot can take one's own meager plot into itself. And the yearning is that from that point, the lonely "I" pronouns will become "we." Home is the name.

This Story within a story is what liturgy is all about. The purpose of worship is so to portray *the* Story that, at least for its duration, one participates in an alternative world that rivals the daily living that society provides. With all the means at a faith community's command, space and time need to be so sacralized within its liturgy that all of life is claimed as enfolded within it. When liturgy is done at its best, persons will stumble out from the Sunday worship into their ordinary world, uncertain as to which "world" is the real one. In another sense, liturgy is rehearsal, preparing people to live that plot in distinct contrast to the secular liturgy that informs one's work-a-day world. The situation is not that of "liturgies" contrasted with "no liturgies." Whatever one does and wherever one goes, the liturgy of the Christian is in contest with secular liturgies. Since we are people of habit, we are always being formed in one way or another. Our fallen condition encourages us to fill our space with noise and things, with *time* clocked by Internet usage or portioned off in TV's half-hour blocks.

Deep within each of us is one or more *obsessios.* These are dangerous memories that haunt us with tapes during the day and open doors in our soul at night. That which can heal, or at least sublimate, these *obsessios* we call *epiphania,* which means "gracious hints." One's pilgrimage is a dynamic fluctuation between these two poles. One can mark as tragic the life in which the *obsessios* are so strong as to devour any gracious hints of affirmation that may occur. When the *epiphania* are powerful enough to contain the *obsessios,* we experience "salvation," which means "to make healthy and whole," just as when a grain of sand intruding into an oyster becomes a pearl. Out of this dynamic emerges a primal image that informs one's pilgrimage with coherence and consistency. In turn, the plot one identifies provides the particular flavor by which the doctrinal questions are "posed" and the manner in which one perceives the "answers."[2]

Most of us take time each month to balance our checking account, comparing canceled checks with the bank statement, determining whether we have overspent or if there is a reserve in the account. This is precisely what we need to do as well in spiritual terms. In fact, the checkbook itself can provide a handy way for determining one's priorities. It is also a barometer for perceiving balance in one's life, by observing the interplay of money spent for self and others, for enjoyment and for learning, for those most in need or those comfortably close by. One also needs to peruse one's daily calendar to discern one's approach to time. Such a process the Church has called a time of "recollection," rendering self-conscious how one spends one's *time* and fills one's *space*. "What's the bottom line?" is a question often asked. Here one asks it of one's life.

9. Faith as Need and Promise

Faith begins in need. As St. Rose of Lima insisted, "Without the burden of afflictions, it is impossible to reach the height of grace." So frequently do we deceive ourselves into self-aggrandizement, however, that our only hope is that our inflated posture will be punctured. A pundit once observed that we pray best in the dentist's chair. Ernest Becker insists that we must come to understand ourselves as dependent fugitive creatures sharing the same limitations and inheriting the same half-animal past.

One characteristic, however, that separates us from the rest of the animal kingdom is our *capacity to make and keep promises*. In fact, the heart of the Old Testament rests on this theme. Its plot is a divine-human covenant enacted as gift, continually countered by Israel's penchant for faithlessness in the face of the divine promise. In my own pilgrimage, I was early drawn to the theology of Karl Barth.

I understand now that, in the light of my struggle with my mother, I liked Barth because my seminary professor said, "For Barth, God is the One who makes and keeps promises." Even on a purely human level, Nietzsche defines a person as "that animal who makes promises." And so is the affirmation of the psalmist: "Your promise gives me life." And again, "If you uphold me by your promise, I shall live" (Ps. 119, v. 50, v. 116 GRAIL). As we will discover, the primary disclosure of God in the Eucharist is based on Promise.

10. Christian Doctrines

The Christian doctrinal answers to the common questions center on declaring Jesus to be the Incarnation of God, and regarding the Christ event as the poem that God made, as Oscar Wilde called it. St. Bernard of Clairvaux regarded Jesus' entire life as God's parable. Each Gospel writer discloses a different facet of this parable, like the surfaces of an exquisitely cut diamond radiating with a mysterious beauty. The only Jesus we have is the remembered one, and that is all we need. *What matters for Christians is the testimony of thankful remembrance by those who through Jesus have experienced transformation.* The foremost question today is not the existence of God. It is the power of Jesus to transform lives—a radical change that is to the self what Pentecost is to the Church, both of which are to be celebrated as spiritual birthdays. The deeper the Holy Spirit is experienced, the more unquenchable one's thirst to participate in the final unity of all things in God. And the more this Spirit opens us to the various perspectives and nuances of the Christ event, the more multicolored Christ's impact becomes—an event wild and brilliant.

We have been concerned with the universal questions in terms of which Christian doctrine is distilled and in turn acted out as liturgy. As one lives this process, a primal image emerges as both the ground and the conclusion of one's living. Finally this image functions as spectacles by which one perceives the relation between self and world. While we have affirmed imagination as a primary way in which to distill one's world of time and space, Christian doctrines are answers that serve as markers for each of us, as well as informing the Church's own pilgrimage. In both cases the questions invite the imagination to explore and expand the doctrinal meaning. Neither self nor Church dare stray far from the questions themselves. And these questions mount toward the Doctrine of doctrines—that of *God*.

Let us summarize, as preparation for the chapters that follow, how these doctrines may look as a basis for understanding a Christian approach to time and space. God is the length, breadth, height, and depth, everywhere and in everything, as both source and end. In Jesus Christ as the one who is for us and with us, the fathomless and silent Mystery is given a face and a name. His incarnation is a disclosure of God's choice to take up residence within us, and it also discloses that God's perspective functions from the bottom up, and God's judgment operates from the top down. Our response of faithful living is best understood not so much in terms of God's *will*, but as participating in God's *yearning*. To be touched by this divine craving is to hear the unspeakable Voice calling us beyond ourselves, serving as the horizon of our being. "Kingdom" (or reign) is the promise given to us as overwhelming gift, so grand that one is thankful even for the invitation into self-sacrifice. Each of us is called to contribute to the earth as a member of Christ's body, for whom the Church in the world is Christ's heart. Above all, it is in the Eucharistic gesture that we encounter finally *the primal image*—the promise that the works of our hands and the feelings of our souls are lifted up into God, anticipating the final consummation in which Christ shall make oblation to the Father, and time and space will pass fully into God. Heaven is everywhere, experienced as momentary foretastes, whetting our yearning all the more for union with God. This vision rests upon the divine promise that "while they dance, they will sing: 'In you all find their home'" (Ps. 87:7 GRAIL). Living with these understandings provides a new way of seeing.

Even difficult doctrines such as "hell" can best be understood in terms of one's primal image. "Hell" is like spending eternity where everyone is laughing and we do not get the joke. Or more seriously, hell is the experience of spending one's life losing God and experiencing the inexpressible pain of his absence. In this life, hell means living without the Presence. But "purgatory" is the more apt term for such an existence, for divine love keeps "hell" open. Without the opportunity of "practicing eternity," how can Hitler ever learn to embrace the Jews as his friends? Soelle would have us know that the Christian pilgrimage can destroy persons, drive them mad, make them ill, and bring them to ruin. Christian faith is a life-and-death enterprise, for it is all or nothing.

11. Jesus Christ and the Church

Above all other doctrines, the sacralizing of time and space centers in an intense love affair with Jesus.[3] Jesus is God and human, our redeemer, savior, perfect person, whole person, a person beautiful, holy, complete, fulfilled. He is a poet, mystic, dreamer, savant, leader, and teacher—even our older brother. He lived, taught, suffered, died, rose, and ascended—a path to which he leads and calls us. Jesus would have us be with him, in living and dying, in rising and ascending. Christ is wedded to the whole human family as bride, and unless you are willing to take the whole human family to your own heart, he will have no part of you. Jesus calls all to suffer and die with him and for him.

The Church is Jesus' continued presence on earth. This Church is his spouse, intimate and close, chosen, elected, ravished by his love for her, and through her for all. Unless you have a passionate love for Holy Church, the bride of Christ, it might be better not to come close. Christ's life flows through her into the whole world. The Church is a great mystery, but it is first of all a great love. We are called to grow in love for her, for Christ's life in her and through her. His life in the Church is sustained by his Body and Blood. For this Lord we would gladly die, as for him we gladly and joyously live. Christ must be the beginning of our day and its end. Christ is the point of the Christian life, its core and purpose. Without him, it is just a pious exercise. But with him it is a love affair without parallel this side of eternity. It is amid this love affair that the primal image emerges, by which we see, understand, and function in the sacralizing of time and space.

110

We have spoken of the Mystery of mysteries and the Doctrine of doctrines. In something of the same fashion, the monastery functions as the Church of churches, as a model for Christian life and for the whole Church. Particularly indicative of Christian spirituality are the characteristics the monk Matthew Kelty identifies as necessary for monks as well. Christian spirituality is a call for people who wonder, who can muse and ponder and mull over the Mystery. These are the folks who love the night, and know the moon, and listen to birds sing, and watch the wind in the grass on the hill. They are the lovers of music, who sometimes can play as well. They are the ones who notice the rain, feel the wind, and smell the soup. They are the ones who know what to pray for. And so we pray with them:

> Lord, be *within* me to empower me, be *without* me so that I can endure, *over* me as a shelter, *beneath* me as a support, *before* me as my light, *behind* me to call me back, and throughout, *enfold* me as my Lover.

CHAPTER FIVE

Expansive Time

"For a thousand years in your sight are like yesterday when it is past."
(Ps. 90:4)
"[God] gives to all [the stars] their names." (Ps. 147:4)

1. Relativity of Time

A well-known scriptural image concerning time is this: "With the Lord one day is like a thousand years, and a thousand years are like one day" (2 Pet. 3:9). This implies that both God and we are involved in *time,* but from different perspectives. Time is dependent on the particular stance of the *one who is experiencing it.* In addition, the perception of time also differs depending on what particular activity *is happening* to a particular person during that time. Time is also relative to the *perspective of the primary group* to which one belongs, and which one thus brings to everything perceived. The combination of these factors is what makes the Christian experience time in a way quite different from the non-Christian.

The Christian perceives time differently in two ways. First, it is fundamental to have the *"mind of Christ."* This does not mean having the thinking ability of this first-century dusty peasant. Paul puts it well: "Let the same mind be in you that was in Christ Jesus . . . emptied . . .

112

humbled . . . obedient" (Phil. 2:5-8). To be *emptied* is to see with the perspective of the Holy Spirit, who has taken up residence in the Christian. To see *humbly* is to see life as Jesus did, as a servant to the world. To see *obediently* is to relate to all things not as one might desire, but as Jesus did, obeying the ongoing will or craving of God. Jesus summarizes this unique way in which the Christian relates to all things: "You shall love the Lord your God with all your heart, and with all your soul, and with all your strength, and with all your mind; and your neighbor as yourself" (Luke 10:27). While these dimensions of faith might be regarded as four separate functions, the Christian is directed to use them as a unit—a way best called "faith."

Secondly, the Christian must learn more than *how* to see. "The peace of God which passes all understanding, will guard your hearts and your minds *in* Christ Jesus" (Phil. 4:7; emphasis added). Authentic faith must operate from *within* Jesus as the Christ. The result is a unique way not only of *understanding* time, but also of actually *being* in time. To be a Christian requires that one so experience the sacredness of time as it intersects with space that the very environment in which one lives and moves and has one's being becomes "holy ground." To the degree that Christians live time in this way, to that degree is the coming of the endtime hastened, even though it is always at hand.

Through the centuries, the Church has intertwined this unique *how to see* with *how to be* in a particular activity known as *liturgy.* Liturgy is the intense distillation of the implications of living with Jesus Christ as the center point of time. Some people today see as presumptuous the use of B.C. and A.D., as if these designations force everyone to function by "Christian time." However this issue is resolved, it can hardly be questioned that for the Christian there are far-reaching ramifications for living time from the perspective of a Christological center. Our concern in this chapter and the next is to explore how this relativity of perspective transforms *time* in various ways for the Christian.

Central to the Christian understanding of time is the issue of "duration." It refers to the state or *quality* of living in time. For example, after the two-minute warning in football the defending team feels as though the time will never end; yet those two minutes seem incredibly short for the team that must score in order to win or put the game into "overtime," an interesting word in itself. Duration depends heavily upon subjective dimensions of experience, composed of the various perspectives that we have named.

To summarize, *how* time is experienced depends on the *who* that is experiencing, the *what* that is being done at the time, the *with whom* one stands to see, and the *in* or *where* as the environment or context for the seeing. Each of these becomes different and unique when one becomes a faithful Christian. As over against clock time, Christian time is lived with a sensitivity to "pregnant time"—time ripe and full and expectant, as the Spirit intersects it. Time, understood spiritually, measures not the motion of matter but the activity of spirit. This subjective nature of time is suggested in the daily language we use about time, for example, *find* time, *kill* time, *make* time, *do* time. In fact, many of us will testify that time goes *faster* the longer we live.

Put another way, *duration* is *time as lived*. In the past, such time was taken for granted. Farming as a primary vocation means one divides time by seasons. This is different from calendar time, which is an arbitrary mathematics of time. Rather, seasons entail duration, and thus we can legitimately speak of an "early spring," or a "late fall." This use of adjectives reflects variables even within seasonal time. Planting and harvesting never occur on the same dates, nor does the first snow. Time here is a matter of anticipation, in which looking up at the sky is the foremost way of knowing this time. It is not uncommon to attach such time to things, as in seeing certain characteristics of animal coats and the color of certain woolly worms as harbingers of what and when. The legendary *Farmer's Almanac* is characteristic of this way of telling time.

Immanuel Kant, one of the great Western philosophers, ushered in our modern understanding of time by observing that both time and space are located within the person. It is not a large step from there to affirm that being a Christian entails intense *formation,* whereby time and space as biologically experienced are transformed by becoming rich and qualitatively different because of the Christian's unique perspectives. We can thus speak of "sacred time," meaning experiencing a segment of time not chronologically but in terms of its meaning. Kant later invited this possibility by affirming that while the "reason" cannot have any immediate and direct experience of God, yet the "idea" serves as a channel marker for bringing coherence to one's thinking. The Christian goes even further, insisting that Christianity is a unique way of seeing. It is a multiple perspective that is forged within one's very senses through one's participation in the Church as the Body of Christ. It is through liturgy in particular that one's sensitivity is honed to see in a transformed way. Things become powerful symbols. The Christian actually sees strangers in a different way—as the one for whom Christ died. Daybreak is literally seen as resurrection, and nightfall can become close to a literal dying into the arms of God. The Christian sees and smells and feels and hears and tastes as a poet, in which all of reality is a poem in which one has become immersed. It is hard to overstress the centrality of formation for the Christian, for it must compete daily with the societal formation surrounding us everywhere. Liturgy is a primal way in which time can be rehearsed into disclosing the meaning of all Time.

Powerful illustrations of such liturgical formation are the one hour of Sunday worship, or the monastic way of celebrating everything in one day, or the Church's understanding of the church year. Each of these segments can become transparent, subsumed under cosmic time, not as timelessness but as promised fulfillment.

2. Kairos and Chronos

Different notions of time can be classed according to two contrasting images: that of being *timely* (*kairos*) and that of being *prompt* (*chronos*). In contrast to *kairos* as the fullness or pregnancy of time, the industrial revolution introduced *chronos* time almost everywhere. The invention of the portable clock replaced the *kairos* of diverse seasons as revealing the meaning of time. Before the advent of clocks, one could function according to the rhythms of anticipation and satisfaction, or planting and harvesting, each marked by "rightness" or "ripeness." This contrast can be expressed in another way, as the "prepared moment" *(kairos)* versus the "correct moment" *(chronos)*. The precision of the metronome replaced, in effect, the rhythms of the body. As a result, we have largely lost touch with organic rhythms, such as birth, maturation, and death, which formerly governed all of life. *Wisdom* is a word that Scripture uses to indicate the ability to sense timeliness and appropriateness. "For everything there is a season, and a time for every matter under heaven" (Eccles.3:1).

In modern life, with its wholesale emphasis on the economic, efficiency becomes the measure of time. What matters is how long it takes to accomplish a task, and this mindset leads to assembly lines, with shifts rigidly regulated by the clock—with the result that work is often shoddy. As a result, one's life becomes a string of years that have lost almost any identifying characteristics. The only recognizable markers come from society, when at age sixteen one has attained the age needed for obtaining a driver's license, at twenty-one one can legally drink, and at sixty-five one can retire to count grandchildren. The years in between become memorable through such events as sports (the year the Royals won the pennant) or crisis (the year of the big flood). Even the origins of the three summer holidays have become so meaningless that the dates of two of them appear on Mondays so we can have longer weekends. Christmas and Easter are fairly well bereft of religious meaning for the general populace, with Santa Claus and the Easter Bunny holding center stage. And sooner or later, children come to realize that they have been duped, even by the tooth fairy, and they begin to question other stories that claim to be disclosures of meaning. Even the legendary Christmas "Midnight Mass" has been changed in many churches to an earlier time, no longer determined by meaning and mystery,

117

but by convenience. It may be that the natural variability of a woman's period is one of the few organic times remaining, yet pills permit tampering even there.

From time to time, monasteries have provided a much-needed revival of sensitivity to sacred time in the Church. Monastic time is sacralized time, made possible because the monastery is totally separate from society's dynamics, and thus has total freedom to restructure time according to religious meaning. As we will explore later, religious orders such as the Trappists divided the number three, because of the Trinity, into the twenty-four hours of clock time, resulting in eight "offices" or periods of time, each with a separate name and worship.[1] Together these offices permit the monk or nun in one "sun day" to participate in the whole of salvation time and its history. Jesus called for the Christian to live one day at a time. Monastics do. The result is glorious. One receives a fresh day at every sunrise and celebrates the resurrection. At sundown, the monastic returns the day to God and hopes he or she has used his or her talents as gifts for God. Then, making one's "final" peace with the world, the monastic enters the "death of sleep" with the words of Jesus, "Into your hands, Lord, I commend my spirit."

Monastic time likewise turns the secular understanding of *work* on its head. One does not labor to finish a job, as if work is a matter of scratching things off a list, wanting nothing more than to get them done. Instead, labor at the monastery is a process whereby the task is done joyfully for its own sake as a gift to God—even scrubbing the toilets. One's work ends with the sound of the bells calling each person to chapel to offer one's gift. These periodic times of worship help the monastic remember that the gift that God prizes is characterized not by the "what" or the "how much," but by the "how." Truly to live for God is what monastic life attempts, and by example the monastery helps the Church to see how significantly different Christian time is from that of society.

Such an understanding of time is meant not just for those called to the monastic life. In the early Middle Ages people built their homes around the monastery. The *Angelus* was rung every day, at early morning, noon, and night. When it was heard, the peasants would pause in their work to pray. In fact, until recent times, parish lines were marked by how far the church bell could be heard. At Vespers, the villagers would come to the church, for there was the only candle that burned at all times. From this they lit their evening candles and returned thankfully to their homes.

3. Cosmic Time

Although *liturgy* is interpreted and understood in many ways, perhaps it is best understood as a sacralization of time, in its broadest and most inclusive sense. Many are the times that we cry out, "What's it all about?" In our preoccupation with keeping our body alive, or providing shelter sufficient for one's family, the danger is that we will lose any perspective broader or deeper than one's own autobiography. Yet during the midnight hours, many of us are forced to ask, "Is this all?" As a character in Samuel Beckett's *Waiting for Godot* confides: "They give life astride the grave." Is there any meaning beyond worry and tomorrow's peanut-butter-and-jelly sandwich?

The need for liturgy becomes clearer when one consults one's overbooked schedule. Just as monthly "recollections" ask if there is anything left, liturgy is the event by which we appraise our life: our time, space, money, relationships, shortcomings, vision, temptations, and hopes. Liturgy is akin to drama, as a rehearsal of cosmic time. It reenacts the widest panorama conceivable, from primal beginning to wide-eyed consummation. It is the telling and living out of an image powerful enough to subsume one's daily and weekly and monthly and yearly and lifelong times into a whole that smiles with meaning. As evangelism it is the invitation to compare stories. If one's plot resonates with *the Story,* one has come home. Liturgy is a portrayal of living the Mystery between memory and vision.

One attends church not just when one feels like it, but even more when one doesn't—when one has lost the way, or forfeited the larger picture, or been seduced by a distraction. Nowhere is the subversive nature of the Church more apparent than in its liturgy. Our society promises power as a reward for hard work, prestige for those who climb the ladder, and possessions to pamper the most fastidious of tastes. Christianity is a story of the contrary—for in the Christian world the first are in fact last, the rich go away empty, and death buries us all. What is more pathetic than those who realize too late that they cannot take with them anything for which they have toiled a lifetime?

Cosmic time refers to the most inclusive, expansive, deepest rhythm, in which all of time and space are included. It can be sensed in such a thought as, "Is the Universe compassionate?" In Scripture, cosmic time takes its meaning as that toward which the whole process of God's activity intends. In a number of ways, this kind of time gives rise to the image of all things moving toward a finale when God shall be "all in all" (1 Cor. 15:28). And in so being, the meaning of each part is that God may be everything to every one. "The creation itself will be set free from its bondage to decay and will obtain the freedom of the glory of the children of God. We know that the whole creation has been groaning in labor pains until now. . . . For in hope we are saved" (Rom. 8:21-22, 24).

To understand this most inclusive grasp of time, liturgy is our primary resource. Liturgy is faith ignited by imagination into symbolic action, enabling the gospel to become flesh. Liturgy is a way of understanding by singing from one's heart. Put best, liturgy is the lens through which time is transfigured in the light of its promised consummation. Carl Braaten understands this well in his *Christ and Counter-Christ,* seeing that the total span of both cosmic and personal time are being drawn into God. This includes the stars and the planets, the winds and the waves, the rocks and the flowers, the animals and humans, in the event of "total salvation." So it is that Nicolas Berdyaev in *The Destiny of Man* even includes every blade of grass in the cosmic fulfillment.

Cosmic time as the "big picture" gains much from present-day cosmology. With every new image from the Hubble telescope, I become increasingly fascinated by the deep sense of the mystery of it all. The cosmos is so vast that we have only mathematical signs to express it, and they point toward dimensions that are utterly inconceivable. How is one to know what to do with something whose observed depth at this moment is in terms of fifteen billions of light-years? The scientific theory most accepted at present for the miracle of creation is that of the "Big Bang." Here we are invited to entertain the incredible Mystery of an "infinite center," smaller than a pinpoint, that at one particular moment billions of years ago, in one incredible act of infinite expansion, gave birth to the entire cosmos—and continues to do so. Such a "beginning" from an infinitesimally small point suggests a point of Infinite Depth.

As if such an ongoing act of creation doesn't plunge us deeply enough into Mystery, even more incredible is that through this enormous process of time, living creatures now abound. Still more miraculous, humans have emerged as creatures who are not only self-conscious, but can look back over the whole process in order to understand how this birthing takes place. The entire cosmic process has come to an amazing threshold, in which love is born in what was formerly savage. And the lover can grasp the universe as birthed by love and as moving toward a loving resolution. Even the fact that "spirituality" has emerged is miraculous—that there are a number of people who consciously commune with Consciousness and dare to claim love as the motivation of the Infinite Center of the universe. The key to this magnificent whole is the movement from nothingness toward the divine emergence as "all in all." The birth of the cosmos, as God's ongoing self-consciousness, is the beginning of time as relationship. Thus, although God and humans are involved differently *with* time, it is *in* time that they meet. "A thousand ages in your sight are like an evening gone," says the hymn "O God Our Help in Ages Past."

Teilhard de Chardin has related his scientific study of paleontology to the meaning of cosmic time. Perhaps his greatest contribution is a "language" by which one's imagination is lured toward imagery that is fresh with cosmic meaning. For example, some of the phrases he uses to grasp the reality blunted by the overused word "God" are as the:

indomitable quest for fuller being
spiritual residue of every suffering and diminishment
final center of convergence toward Spirit
relentless drive toward increased consciousness and love
blessed intoxication of a transfigured humanity
definitive liberation of matter into spirit
omnipresence in the vast regions of the cosmos
love that is the determined drive for transcendence
vital current of human development
mysterious force sustaining all things
irrepressible dynamism of the cosmos in evolution
fundamental impulse of all life
free outpouring of the spirit
exhilarating accent to cosmic consciousness

The Christian's story begins not simply with one's birth, but with the cosmos itself. In worship, the Eucharist is a drama in which we pass through all of time, from beginning to consummation. And this end, in turn, flows back over the whole, disclosing the character of every part. But to be grasped by such an astonishing drama, one must be awakened, often by disappointment or tragedy, which either brings one to despair or enables one to loosen control on one's little world and instead open oneself to residing in Mystery. It is helpful here to distinguish between Eucharistic and non-Eucharistic worship. The Eucharist can best be seen as a lens for understanding cosmic time.

Non-Eucharistic worship we will develop as one way of entering eternal time.

In the early Church, *laos* (laity) meant all the people of God. *Cleros* was the "inheritance" for which the laity was responsible. In time, *cleros* came to mean "clergy," and it is they who became responsible for preserving the inheritance. Understood either way, the "inheritance" bequeathed to the Church gathers around a "primal image." A primal image is one that can best hold the meaning of the whole, from cosmic time to the smallest dimension of momentary time. It is my perception that the image that the Church through the centuries has most celebrated as best imaging this whole is the *Eucharistic gesture*. In other words, the lifting up of the bread and wine as the Body and Blood of Christ in the Eucharist distills the movement of all time. As we will later explore, this gesture emerges centrally from the three most sacred days of the Church year: the *Triduum* (Maundy Thursday, Good Friday, and Easter Vigil).

This Eucharistic gesture in present time captures the rhythm of cosmic time from birth to consummation. In response to God's gift of creation, the works of our hands are offered as divine gift, are divinely blessed, and are restored to us as the supreme act of grace, empowering us in vision and strength to respond faithfully again—ever renewed, over and over. In the elevation of the elements in the Eucharist, all is lifted into the divine immensity. As Merton affirmed, "God draws the universe back into himself."

Eucharist is the very nature of the divine-human interchange. As its beginning, present, and future, the divine flows into the finite to restore it. We ourselves are a project of God's making, and the works of our hands are the gifts through which we joyously lose ourselves in God. The heart of this Christian understanding of cosmic time appears in the liturgy for the Easter Vigil. As the present year is carved into the huge Easter candle, these words are said: "Christ yesterday and today, the beginning and the end, Alpha and Omega; all time belongs to him and all the ages; to him be glory and power through every age forever." This is cosmic time.

The Catholic Mass is not the only liturgy that can serve to form a person in cosmic time. So does the powerful cosmic portrayal in the liturgy in the Orthodox Church, for example as in "The Divine Liturgy of St. John Chrysostom." As Fr. Alkiviades Calivas put it, "The Divine Liturgy is a complex act of movement, sound, and sights," characterized by "a deep sense of harmony, beauty, dignity, and mystery."[2] Verbal and nonverbal elements together enrich the Church as the glorious Body of Christ itself. While the structure of the Roman Catholic Mass focuses on a rhythm of forgiveness and sanctification, the Orthodox focus is more eschatological: The participant is already being immersed in a glorious foretaste of the heavenly kingdom. Resurrection, Ascension, enthronement, and the glorious Second Coming—these are central in drawing us into cosmic time. Past, present, and future are intertwined with Promise as the essence of all meaning, experienced as anticipation. Promise is what glues all things together in glory. Nothing appears as it is now, but as everything shall become. The "now" becomes richer, however, as the presence of God's consummation invades our time. In the Christ event, Mystery enters time, so that all of time might enter into the ultimate Mystery.

The Anglican *Book of Common Prayer* stands as a classic expression of what we are affirming as cosmic time, as well as of eternal time, to which we turn next. The former is beautifully expressed in the liturgy for the Holy Eucharist. The latter is evident in the Daily Office for Morning and Evening Prayer.

4. Eternal Time

We have explored cosmic time and space as the huge picture. Its concern is with the enormous movement of the whole toward consummation, as graphically portrayed in the Eucharistic gesture. This gesture is that of offering up to God and into God the works of our hands and the being of our living, having it returned, blessed, and restored. This we take into ourselves as grace and gift, empowered once again to invest our talents according to God's cravings, lifting again the works of our hands into God, again and again. To touch this choreography of the spheres in any way is to be reduced to shy humility, for one can easily become lost in the depth of cosmic time.

When we turn now to eternal time, our perspective remains large, but becomes a bit more contained and focused. Instead of being swept by the cosmos, our attention becomes global, concerned for the earth, for the planet we call home. Cosmic time is more spherical, eternal time more linear. There is a before and after, a past, present, and future. Every novel is based upon a plot, with the suspense depending on how long it takes for the reader to "catch on" to what the characters do not yet see. So it is in every life. The question "why?" is so deeply implanted in us that we cannot live without a plot, even if that plot is only hinted. Without one, life is like clinging to the end of a frayed rope. Plot, in the sense that we are using the term, is not reasoned out, nor does it signify actions issuing from rational conclusions. Rather, a plot lays hold of a person. It is usually discovered later in life and reveals a meaning that has been operative since the womb. A question fundamental to eternal time is whether one's plot is "given," in part or as a whole, or whether it is "self-created." That is, are there any "givens" to life, or is life "free floating?" This question became a rich conflict between two "existentialists," Soren Kierkegaard, a Christian, and Jean-Paul Sartre, for most of his life an "atheist." Sartre insisted on total freedom, even if the result is often tragic. Since there is no God, individuals do not have an *essence* that they need to become. Rather, life is the task of providing an "essence" for oneself, with authenticity the mark of how well the individual is faithful to the "essential life" that one has chosen. Kierkegaard disagreed, insisting that since there is a Creator God, we have an ascribed essence that we are to become, in faithfulness to the one who created us. Kierkegaard's analogy is that the self is much like the seed of a maple tree. It is so formed interiorly that it has no other "choice" but to be a maple tree. Thus even if we can conceive of that seed being given freedom, all that would mean is either that it chooses to be a glorious maple tree, or a stunted maple, dying in the self-destroying dynamic of denying what it is. *So it is with each person.*

The Christian would see as a self-destructive tragedy the plot of someone who, in denying God, denies themselves as innately formed and intended by the Creator. The plot of history is the movement from "rebellion" through "crucifixion" to "resurrection" in newness of life. Dostoyevsky's *The Brothers Karamazov* is one of the greatest Christian novels. To make sure that the reader doesn't miss his primal motif, he provides at the beginning a quotation from Scripture, the theme on which all his works are variations: "Verily, verily, I say unto you, except a corn of wheat fall into the ground and die, it abideth alone; but if it die, it bringeth forth much fruit" (John 12:24).[3] Crucifixion and resurrection is the plot of the Christ event, and thus, one way or another, is the theme for all humanity. While the plot of each person's life is somewhat different, depending on the particulars, there is also a fundamental commonality in all human life. Dostoyevsky held that to know the "master plot," one had to live as if there were none, and it is through the misuse of freedom that one discovers, often tragically, the limits within which self and history are bound to struggle. Eternal time lays claim to the relationship between the Eternal (i.e., God) and the human struggle as a historical whole and reveals *the pilgrimage of humankind.*

Similarly, to understand Judaism one has to come to terms with the Exodus. Jewish history consists of multiple variations on the theme of God's choosing Israel as a special people, followed by Israel's unfaithfulness, and finally God's merciful restoration; on and on that plot continues. The plot of Luke's Gospel is told in three consecutive parables in chapter fifteen: the Lost Sheep, the Lost Coin, and the Lost Son. Whether we are likened as sheep, money, or prodigal son, Luke's key motif is clear. God is the one who plays lost and found, and eternal time can be likened to the prodigal son drama as the nature of the interaction between God and humankind.

Here we are exploring eternal time as a *given,* with which one's "life time" must come to terms. This is analogous to the way in which eternal time, in its own way, must find its place in cosmic time. Only when, for one reason or another, one is stopped in one's tracks, is one then able to hear the basic question: "Why am I doing all this?" When the main character in Franz Kafka's *The Trial* is mysteriously "arrested" on his birthday, the only identification he can find is his bicycle license. What can any of us show as a sign of a larger plot on which one's own plot might depend? Much of our floundering is about being "arrested" by the possibility that there is a macrocosm for our microcosm, in terms of which our pilgrimage might make sense.

There is an answer for those who question going to church when they might better find God in the fresh greenness of a golf course. What we need, and sometimes desperately so, is to step out of the mire of our daily tedium, to have our perspective renewed by entering a world rendered sacred by being structured by eternal time. This is what can bequeath to our "ordinary time" a nonordinary, even an extraordinary, meaning.

A church group assigned to plan a worship service often falls into an interesting dynamic. The members usually begin by identifying "ingredients" characteristic of worship: hymns, prayers, Scripture. The difficulty often arises in knowing how to assemble these parts. Perhaps the most important feature of worship is its *structure*—its choreography, as it were. When structure is not a first priority, the result can be like arbitrarily scrambling the acts and scenes of a play. Structure is characteristic not only of "liturgical worship;" even within the free-church tradition a "regular" order usually emerges in practice.

The choreography characteristic of much non-Eucharistic worship is eternal time. Its purpose is the recital of God's acts in history on our behalf. This divine-human exchange usually prefers the spoken word, in contrast to the preference in Eucharistic worship for the acted sign. Although the structure is not always apparent, it tends to reflect the implicit structure of Scripture itself. In his book *The Unfolding Drama of the Bible*, Bernhard Anderson provides a structure that is helpful not only in understanding Scripture, but also in understanding the foundation that is often implicitly characteristic of non-Eucharistic worship. He identifies both a Prologue and an Epilogue, between which are three main acts, characterized by two scenes each:[4]

> Prologue: "In the Beginning"—theme of Creation and
> Rebellion as "Paradise Lost"; human roles as
> Gardener, Rebel, finally Fugitive
> Act One: The Formation of God's People
> Scene One: Exodus—freedom from Egypt, Red Sea
> escape, making of covenant
> Scene Two—Exile as punishment
> Act Two—The Re-formation of God's People
> Scene One: Second Exodus
> Scene Two: Legalism
> Act Three—The Transformation of God's People
> Scene One: Jesus Christ—Incarnation and the
> scandal of the Cross
> Scene Two: The Church in the World
> Epilogue: A New Heaven and Earth

These three key acts in God's dealings with humanity express the Christian panorama of Exile/Exodus, or Crucifixion/Resurrection. Each act, in turn, is structured as variations on a central theme: God's gift, human rebellion, God's gracious forgiveness, God's promised vision. This is the *corporate* theme that serves well for understanding the structure and meaning of most Protestant worship.

This structure correlates well with the identifiable parts of Isaiah's vision of God in the Temple (Isa. 6:1-8), which expresses the same theme for an *individual.* The first element is adoration ("Holy, Holy, Holy"), the second is confession ("Woe is me!"), the third is affirmation ("Your guilt has departed"), and the fourth is dedication ("Here am I; send me!"). Thus the four movements of individual worship or pilgrimage correlate with the structure of Christian history, as it can be recognized in public worship as the drama of eternal time. *Adoration* is rooted in *creation, confession* as our response to the *Fall, affirmation* centers in the *Christ event,* and *dedication* is our promise to act on behalf of the *Kingdom.* Most Protestant worship can be identified in terms of this model. In the schema below on the left are the historical themes as events: *creation,* human rebellion as the *Fall,* Jesus Christ as God's decisive act on our behalf, and the *Kingdom of God* as the promise for the future. This rhythm is repeated throughout history. On the right is the correlating activity in worship, providing a recognizable structure. Thus in non-Eucharistic worship, the pilgrimage of history in its sweep correlates with the pilgrimage of each Christian in its particularity.

Creation—Adoration
Fall—Confession
Jesus as the Christ—Affirmation
Kingdom of God—Dedication

Years ago I saw the play *Hair* in Montreal. I was never sure when the play actually started. As the audience began to assemble, there were stagehands and various people climbing on the scaffolding that projected into the seating, or checking lights and donning costumes. We were drawn into whatever was going to be, complete with my being asked to hold the end of an extension cord while someone taped it. So, in its own way, is the beginning of worship in mainline Protestant churches. It is called "Prelude." This is not to be a display of the organist's talent. The music should be chosen as carefully as if one were filming a motion picture. The mood is that of expectant waiting, as the Spirit passes softly over the void of Nothingness, the earth still a void, without form, awaiting the divine act (Gen. 1:1). There is really no precise place of beginning, except perhaps a voice is heard, calling for Light, a pushing back by God, so that the darkness is gathered into night, and God's giving light to form the day. God saw that it was good, very good. One can use slides or other ways of participating in the full beginning of the majestic beauty of God's acts of Creation. The gathering or opening hymn should be one of joy over God's creation, such as "Joyful, Joyful, We Adore Thee" or "For the Beauty of the Earth." The event parallels the emotions of the worshipper. Our response to Creation is, at the beginning, that of *adoration*.

The second "act" is that of the *Fall* (Gen. 3). There is a time of silence, as we too ponder with Adam and Eve our options. Humans are created as the centerpiece of God's glorious creation, called to the happy task of completing creation, as a gardener might bless the landscape. But then, at the pinnacle of our dignity, humans hear the shadowy temptation born from the gift of freedom, "If only you will disobey, you will be as God." Here, as with Adam and Eve, we in effect say to God: "Nice place you have here, God, but just one more thing. We want to own it!" And at that moment, humans fell—and continue to fall. No longer content to be stewards who are privileged to garden the earth into fullness, we turn to exploitation, doing everything for our own self-aggrandizement, leaving creation in shambles. Trees once adorned with colorful leaves now are seen as if they have dollar bills tied to every branch. History takes on its sinister shadows, pitting divine and human as rivals. This happened not only once, but is the major theme of history itself. Kierkegaard once wrote that he did not know why Adam and Eve did what they did, but in hearing what *they* did, he understood why *he* did what he did. One sees the same theme being played out throughout Scripture. The characters change, but the tragic theme stays constant. In the acts and scenes that follow in Scripture, the parts of Adam and Eve are taken next by Cain and Abel, and then Abraham and Isaac—until we reach Jesus and Judas, followed by all the disciples, without exception.

At this point in the "worship plot," having come to a dead end in our rebellion, we hear God's invitation to *confess*. This invitation comes with a dual focus, with both corporate and individual expressions. Jung once said that what most of his clients needed was not a psychiatrist, but a priest. It would not help these persons for the therapist to instruct the clients to stop "guilt-tripping" themselves. What they need is to confess it all and then hear the incredible words of absolution. "Though your sins are as scarlet, you are washed as white as snow." How many millions of individuals yearn to have the slate washed clean! "Confession" has two parts. In the general confession "the church confesses to corporate sin, as well as the

133

participation of each of us in it. Then one dares to enter the profound silence where one faces God in all one's nakedness, asking for personal forgiveness. Confession is not simply for acts committed or omitted, but for the state of one's life—for lusting for power, prestige, and possessions. In a significant sense, forgiveness for Christians is a remembrance of one's baptism and confirmation, now reaffirmed by divine actions. Powerful is the growing tendency in some congregations to sprinkle water on the people, with the words "remember your baptism and be thankful."

With the act of absolution declared, the response of the worshippers is one of joy. This can be expressed in the form of an alleluia or an appropriate psalm of thanksgiving. It is crucial to root this moment of absolution in the promises of Scripture, which may be read at this point. With the awareness that "once I was blind, but now I see," one is prepared to hear the "whence" of one's new life. This is the section identifiable as *affirmation*. The Scripture readings are so chosen that one sees not only one's own self or one's culture in what is read, but one also hears the promise of God. The purpose of the Gospel reading and the sermon that follows is to give the good news a face: "His name is Jesus." In response to Scripture and sermon, we affirm our faith through the creed—which expresses the who and what and why in the Story—with the words "We believe . . . ." In having been restored to health by forgiveness and acceptance, we dare with the prayers of the people to bring to our Redeemer God our hurts, our joys, our hopes, and our dreams for the entire creation.

Act Four, functioning almost as an epilogue, is the stage we can call *dedication*. We dedicate ourselves to the

Kingdom (Reign or Realm of God). This part functions in worship as the equivalent of the final book of the Bible (Revelation). It focuses graphically on the Christian vision of a new heaven and a new earth, where God himself will be with his people, and God will wipe every tear from their eyes and death shall be no more. We have been prepared by the whole drama to be sent out now into the world as co-creators with God in that dream.

Then we reach the benediction or blessing, which is important. Because of the sense of community we experience at worship, it is frightening to be sent alone into the world with the mission to turn everything upside down. In parting from the community of the faithful, we are blessed by the promise of Christ, that though we are separated one from another, through the Holy Spirit in each of us we shall continue to be One. The purpose of the whole drama is to send out faithful workers into the vineyard of God's creation. The recessional or postlude carries through with this theme in triumphant sounds of victory. When participating in worship structured in this way, one stands within the purview of eternal time.

5. Cultural Time

Cultural time is coming into its own with the idea of "indigenization," which means taking seriously the culture in which Christianity participates. Paul Tillich was one of the first thinkers in our time to affirm its importance. He uses three categories, arranged in a sequence that can be prophetic in helping us to understand the edge to which society's value-structure is bringing us. The ideal is *theonomy.* This is a period of time when most things are seen symbolically, as transparent to the Ground of Being. This state makes sense by observing Tillich's distinction between sign and symbol. A *sign* is an arbitrary way of giving something a name for the sake of communicating. A *symbol,* however, is something that has the power to evoke the reality to which it points. A flag is such a symbol, and people fight, and even kill, when their flag is trampled or burned. The Blessed Virgin Mary is such a symbol for Catholics. For Protestants, however, Mary is only a sign, for when she functions as a symbol, Protestants tend to view this as bordering on idolatry. Tillich names most cultural beginnings as being *theonomous*: a time when things are experienced as so resident with power that one must participate in carefully crafted liturgy to ward off any destructive power radiating through things and animals. While each primitive culture shares these characteristics, Tillich names the early Middle Ages as being a significant theonomous time in the West, when the cathedral was the geographic center from which all other activities and institutions took their meaning.

Yet once a theonomous culture begins to have its major symbols "demythologized," the movement toward *autonomy* is inevitable. A culture can exist for a period of time in an autonomous state by living on the borrowed meaning from the theonomous period before, but eventually it will be emptied of meaning and purpose. This is the situation in many countries today, in which the influx of free enterprise desacralizes many objects and roles, depriving them of their intrinsic value. Such is the case in India and Japan.

It is possible to intervene in an effort to put off the inevitability of an autonomy by creating an *heteronomy.*

This is a state in which "meaning" is imposed upon a culture from above. This can be done by dictatorship, as in China; or one-party control, as in efforts by Islamic fundamentalists in the Middle East, or in increasingly restrictive laws, flooding prison population as in the United States.

But while heteronomy can hold off for a while the demise of an autonomous culture, autonomy will inevitably play itself out. The once intrinsic values and sacredness of a culture can no longer feed a nation and its people with meaning. Tillich's contention is that in the ashes of autonomy as "self-sufficient finitude," a new culture may be reborn as a resurrection. This is a period in which new and unexpected values spring forth from the Ground of Being, gushing forth with a power to embrace and unfold a new meaning—such as occurred during the Renaissance, in part. During such a period, theonomous means birth from the bottom up, in heavy contrast to a heteronomous imposition from the top down. It is now well over two generations since Tillich was hopeful for the collapse of the West, in its fullblown autonomy, thereby setting the context for a theonomous breakthrough. He rightly saw a situation in American culture in which our major symbols (religious and secular) have become demythological, placing us on the outer edge of a squandered heritage. But instead of what Tillich hoped, this autonomy has been cloaked over in technological and electronic warp that he could not have imagined rendering our present situation one of growing heteronomy. Whatever names we might identify with this situation, above all what appears to be emerging is a transnational economy whose expressions are indifferent to the cultural meaning of any nation.

We can see from this understanding how Tillich might

understand the Christian faith. Jesus is a theonomous symbol in whose transparency the Ground of Being can be experienced, as the heteronomous hold of self interest is broken in crucifixion. Resurrection is that theonomous state in which, for persons and for a culture, meaning is opened to emerge creatively from beneath. In heavy contrast, however, the present situation in much of the world is one "requiring" a growing military heteronomy to "stabilize" the growing chasm between rich and poor.

6. Historical Time

We are exploring the idea that liturgy and worship provide fundamental patterns and rhythms for our lives. While "cosmic time," "eternal time," and "historical time" are related, the Church through the years has had a hard time giving validity to each. One of the most characteristic tendencies within the Church is to see eternity as timeless, and thus from that perspective history becomes either unreal or condemned by sin to be circular, in effect going nowhere. But in theological quarters today, one of the primary efforts is to relate and connect these dimensions, recognizing and validating authentic *diversity* within the Christian family.

My work in this area has been to explore time as history, and to examine the imagery that informs each person's life. In exploring theology, philosophy, and the arts, I have discerned five "theological worlds" that provide valid options for how Christians view history from the perspective of their own needs.[5] Each of us has a vital issue, basic question, or persistent itch *(obsessio)* that serves as the focus for our life's struggle. It is a complex made of "dangerous memories," whose power is like a "tape" that plays persistently in our living. While there may be more than one, usually they are variations on a basic theme. These are most often rooted in our early, even prenatal, experiences as discussed in Chapter One. This *obsessio* forces one's life into being a pilgrimage: as the search for an *epiphania*. An *epiphania* is a moment of breakthrough, a "gracious hint" that is a "scratch" for one's vexatious itch, an experience posing as potential "answer" for one's gnawing issue. While this pilgrimage is unique to each person, one cannot live without a community of others. In the Church, as well as elsewhere, people cluster, usually with a common *obsessio,* emitting a sense of being "in it together."

A further distinction needs to be made in regard to temperament. *Temperament A* refers to a person whose *obsessio(s)* is so tenacious that most of the time he or she dwells within it, receiving enough *epiphanias* to keep despair at bay. But there is not yet an *epiphania* strong enough to take the *obsessio* into itself. *Temperament B* indicates a person whose *epiphanias* are so deep that she or he can scarcely recall the *obsessio* from which they came. Sin is that state in which one's *epiphanias* are eaten up by one's *obsessios,* not permitting them to give one hope. Redemption is when the *epiphanias* are of such a nature, depth, and frequency that they can embrace the *obsessio* much as answer relates to question. By analogy, the *epiphania* can render an *obsessio* much like an oyster's ability to turn an annoying grain of sand into a pearl. From this perspective, one can look back on one's past, able even to be thankful for some of the wounds that gave rise to one's pilgrimage. Thus while each person is unique, the result of my research is that we can perceive five understandings of history ("worlds"), which result from and in turn give a basic dynamic to one's pilgrimage.

Two books of mine, which we mentioned before, describe in more detail the nature and consequences of these "theological worlds" for the Christian.[6] It is important here simply to indicate the anatomy of these approaches to historical time. Each world is characterized by the interaction of a primal *obsessio* and a primal *epiphania*. While a person can be and usually is involved in more than one world, each person has a "home base" to which one returns for reaffirmation and rest. It is where one "lives."

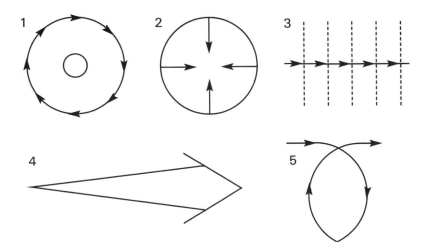

World 1 is the dynamic of *Separation and Reunion*. The issue here is with cosmos, the incredibly vast universe, of sky and electron, so that one has deep sense of longing. As a result, whatever the cause, one's *obsessio* is that of being a stranger, an alien, an orphan; one feels abandoned.

One's *epiphania,* if it occurs, is that of homecoming, with experiences of foretaste. For some persons, this life of faith is of a mystic variety. It is a state that all of us can sense in seeing a vee of birds in the autumn, flying where one cannot go. It may come in watching Judy Garland in *The Wizard of Oz* when she sings, "Birds fly over the rainbow, why then, oh why, can't I." It emerges with tears as one participates in *West Side Story,* when the modern Romeo and Juliet sing, "There's a place for us." In such a view of history, Christ is the one who tears the veil of the temple through which we can catch glimpses of profound Mystery. A defining literary image might be the story of Ulysses, as he struggles to get home. Above all, to live in this world is to be aware of Mystery and of the potentially sacramental nature of all that exists. Here one is close to cosmic history. Favorite hymns are: "I'll Praise My Maker While I've Breath," and "Steal Away." Favorite films are *Star Wars, ET,* and *The Wizard of Oz.*

World 2 is that of *Conflict and Vindication.* The *obsessio* circles around the problem of history itself. Nature is so structured that death permeates everything. Every living thing is supper for someone. And so it is with humans, where from the ghetto to the floor of the stock exchange, competition is fierce, rendering everything in terms of winners and losers. Yet for the Christian, the "feel" is one of anger, for this is not as things ought to be. The *epiphania* that can bring respite is the faith that the God of Scripture takes sides. Yahweh sided with Israel and against Pharaoh, bringing defeat to the Egyptians who oppressed them. So it must be with cancer. Its cause cannot be God's idea, but is instead God's foe—an invasion against which divine and human are pitted. In this historical world, Jesus is the Messiah, the liberator, resembling in everyday life one's older brother or sister who takes one's side. The emphasis in prayer is "Thy Kingdom come, on earth as it is already in heaven." Don Quixote stands as a model. Favorite hymns might include "O Young and Fearless Prophet" or "Where Cross the Crowded Ways," and a favorite film might be *Grapes of Wrath*.

World 3 is *Emptiness and Fulfillment*. The issue evoking this historical world is the dilemma of the *self*. Deep inside, where one's soul purports to be, is the feel of ache, of void. It is reflected in the admonishing we give to children that they should be seen but not heard. Women in our time feel deeply this world. I remember visiting a Rockefeller mansion in which the oak wainscoting on four sides of the dining room in fact hid doors, from which the servants could quietly come to serve and to take away empty plates, disappearing quickly and quietly behind the walls, so that things happen but those who make them happen remain "nonexistent." One feels like an outcast, a second-class citizen—in fact, invisible. The Christian *epiphania* cannot be more sacrificing of one's self for others, for this is what one always does, resulting in an *obsessio* in which one no longer even has a "self" to give away. One seeks rich experiences of "being" and "belonging"—becoming filled to overflowing. Jesus is the model, the pioneer, the example, and the guide. A popular song some years back went "I wish I knew what it's like to be free." In Jesus we do know. He does not do things *for* us (as master to servant) but does things *with* us (as companion). The tragic plot in this world might be Hamlet, in which the dynamic is a Hamlet who could not make decisions, but instead reacted to events. The positive image could be Wagner's *Parsifal*.

Time after time he is the failure of the Round Table, but, by being believed in, he finally succeeds. Favorite hymns might be "Morning Has Broken" or "Breathe on Me, Breath of God." A favorite film might be *Babette's Feast*.

World 4 is that of *Condemnation and Forgiveness*. The issue here is temptation, as one experiences it all around oneself, with a power sufficient, at times, to be called "demonic." The "feel" of the inhabitants in this historical world is that of guilt, a painful awareness of sins that one shamefully hides from others. One feels deserving of condemnation, for from birth onward, the good I would do I do not, and that which I would not do is precisely what I end up doing. St. Paul drew the right conclusions: "There is no health in me." The focus here is not so much on "sins," but on *Sin*—the state out of which sinning comes. Thus our problem is not simply wrong decisions, or getting caught, but of succumbing to the powerful pull of evil, from which one must be delivered. It is a power far greater than I. The literary figure of Faust illustrates this well. In striving to be more than God, he ends up being less than human. Therapists are rarely useful for citizens of this historical world, for most try to get the person to stop feeling as they do. But this is to fail to understand the dynamics at play here. The only *epiphania* that can be healing is one that is a variation on the theme of "Thy sins are forgiven you; take up your bed and walk." Here one longs to be adopted, to be reprieved. Especially powerful is Jesus' promise that God does not treat us as servants, but as heirs, as sons and daughters. Jesus is our Savior, paying the price for us, earning for us the forgiveness of which we are in no way worthy. Members of AA understand this "world," in which God ("a Higher Power") is the One who loves even the slobbering town idiot—and I am he. In literature, none presents this "world" better than Shakespeare's *King Lear,* in which the one who disowns those who love him ends up as the one who through suffering is healed in humility. Appropriate hymns might be "Come Sinners to the Gospel Feast" or "Amazing Grace." Favorite films include *A River Runs Through It, East of Eden, The Fisher King,* and *Field of Dreams.*

World 5 is the world of *Suffering and Endurance.* The issue here is life itself. The "feel" is that of being overwhelmed, on the verge of "too much." I know this view of history from my Appalachian ancestors: the feeling of just making it, fearful that if the rings go out on the car, it will be all over. Another resident of this world might be a rich executive, equipped with ulcer and migraines, for whom the peace of death is tempting. One seems to have the status of victim, of being a refugee. The Christ that can speak to one caught in this *obsessio* is the "the Suffering Servant." He is the one who is with us to the end. "He that shall endure to the end shall be saved." The crucifix can be an evocative symbol, for the One on the cross is God. This is the God who can understand our plight, for he suffers too, and writes off our debt, as it were. The "eucharist" that matters is often one with coffee and friends around a kitchen table. Hymns likely to be heard in this world might be "Must Jesus Bear the Cross Alone" and "How Firm a Foundation." Favorite films might include *Nobody's Fool* and *The Heart is a Lonely Hunter.*

The Church has a firm sense of history, for it knows where home is. Whichever of these five options one most identifies with, one sees it through the eyes of faith as "salvation history"—as sacralized time.

7. Life Time

The phrase "life time" is in current usage, even to the point to which some persons, treating this kind of time quantitatively, see it as preordained. "If your time is up, there isn't anything you can do about it." "I survived World War II because no bullet had my name of it." Perhaps this kind of time is the most haunting, for it becomes personal. There is an ongoing fear running throughout one's life: that one's life has been "much ado about nothing." It might be indicative that in obituaries that I read, a growing number of people no longer have a funeral. What I make out of this is that many persons today no longer have any sense of culmination. Consequently, the day of one's death is not much different from a day of one's life.

How a person incorporates these dimensions of time into one's own ongoing life gives them a particular aura. Life is a pilgrimage, with a beginning and end, although these may be understood in contrasting ways. The first time I self-consciously encountered life as pilgrimage was as a Boy Scout. For close to five years, scouting consumed my prime time. My favorite song was "Trail the Eagle." It was the musical rendition of what the handbook pictured as a zigzag path leading up a mountain. There were a number of arches to pass, where one named one's pilgrimage from beginning as a "Tenderfoot" to climaxing as an "Eagle," the most coveted achievement in scouting. As close as I can remember, this image became the image defining my life for many years. "First the Star, and then the Life, will on your bosom shine." But even though I had fifty-one merit badges, a primal question persisted: "Now what?"

A popular book much read in my parents' day was John Bunyan's *Pilgrim's Progress,* a classic of the Puritan spiritual awakening. It was a graphic allegorical portrayal of the lonely life of a Christian, whom God helps to overcome temptations and birth new attitudes. The pilgrimage was directed to the reward of the "Celestial City." In my day, *The Wizard of Oz* might have served as a secular version. In any case, life is the struggle to "come home," and, as T.S. Eliot said, to see it for the first time.

In our day, some creative connections are being drawn between spirituality and psychology. Assuming that life and people are trustworthy, Erik Erikson developed a neo-Freudian approach, describing stages that together fill the whole life cycle. Each stage calls for a balance between extremes. These stages are as follows: (1) trust vs. mistrust; (2) autonomy vs. shame and doubt; (3) initiative vs. guilt; (4) industry vs. inferiority; (5) identity vs. identity confusion; (6) intimacy vs. isolation; (7) generativity vs. stagnation; and (8) integrity vs. despair. Erikson's work identifies the life cycle in terms of the standard crisis points. His work has been helpful, but the tragedy is that our secular society has hardly any rituals left for giving these crises meaning. And those who have trouble managing this "white water" pilgrimage are called mentally ill and given medication.

Nicolas Berdyaev creatively suggests that every person is a microcosm summing up the whole world. The stages of history are duplicated in each person's stages of growth. Thus, for example, the Renaissance in history is experienced by the self as adolescence, and the modern era might well find correlation with a midlife crisis.

A few other interesting efforts exist to discern in one's lifetime stages that will give meaning to the whole. James

Fowler attempted such an approach, but the result is a needlessly complex naturalism. His effort builds upon the psychological studies of Lawrence Kohlberg and Jean Piaget. Also available are assessment tools for identifying "personality types," differentiating the paths persons will most likely take in finding meaning. The Myers-Briggs Type Indicator, for example, roots such types in positive personal characteristics. The Enneagram, in contrast, differentiates persons according to the way they tend to compensate for their inadequacies.

In the midst of these options, I find particularly interesting Sam Keen's "journey of faith," which consists of five stages.

1. The *Child* lives in the stage of dependence, trained to accept the value structures of both parent and culture.

2. The *Rebel* is the opposite of the first stage, involving counterdependence, a behavior often called "the terrible twos," reappearing during the teens.

3. As an *Adult* one is aware of the goods and evils of the culture, but accepts cooperation as the key virtue. Thus one assumes the social roles characteristic of marriage, work, and consumption as a respectable citizen. The Boy Scout Law summarizes well this stage for Keen.

4. The *Outlaw* Stage is awakened when one's conscience is violated. "Hell no, we won't go" was a sixties version of this stage. The concern here is to discover the self that is almost suffocated by expectations. One's real desires become

unearthed. The old authorities are questioned, as one struggles for self-knowledge. This individual approach, in time, leads one to appreciate how important community can be. Sexuality is an illustration, for it drives one to lose individuality "in the dance of life" and the "ecstasy of being-with."

5. The *Foolish Lover* is characterized by unity and homecoming. For this lover, the world "has ceased to be a problem to be solved and has become a mystery to be enjoyed." One is a fool, for such loving is in spite of everything. This is a later stage, for one cannot give away an ego that is not yet formed. This is to recognize that one cannot teach young people to be saints before they know what it is to be a sinner.[7]

Kierkegaard's existentialist version of three "stages along life's way" is a similar portrait of life time. Stage one is the *aesthetic* stage, characterized by a passion for enjoyment. There are three types illustrating this stage. The seducer refuses any commitment; the tramp refuses to take any vocation; and the professor knows all the options but refuses to adopt an individual point of view. The result in time is insatiable boredom, leading the person to leap out of one untenable stage to another. Second is the *ethical* stage, characterized by a sense of duty. The seducer gets married, the tramp takes a job, and the professor lays claim to a perspective. But in time, this stage of moral existence leads to the awareness of impotence—the good that I would do, I do not . . . .

This dilemma leads to despair, from which one leaps to

the third stage, that of *religiousness*. It takes two forms. Form A occurs when one hears a call higher than the ethical. Kierkegaard's prime example is Abraham, who obeyed when God told him to kill his son. But the result of living in such a stage is that the opposition one encounters with other people leads to a deep sense of guilt. This leads to a dead end, for form B of the religious stage is utterly beyond one's own capacity to choose. In Jesus Christ we encounter the "impossible possibility"—the gospel proclamation that "the Eternal became human." This is totally self-contradictory, much like square pegs in round holes. Consequently, to have faith in the God-man as Incarnation is not something that can arise from within us, but must be that which comes to us. Faith is sheer gift. All one can do to help others travel this life journey is by "wounding from behind," or "pouring salt in open wounds." This pilgrimage is not one in which one jumps positively *to* what may attract one, but one leaps *from* a stage when it is intolerable to remain there.

Whatever image of life time characterizes a particular Christian, that which is held in common is the image of a pilgrimage itself. In some sense or other, there is a start and finish, with an end that flows back over the whole. I see it as one's lifting the entirety as an offering unto God, the wild and fierce divinity, battling against nonbeing in the passion of the One destined to be "all in all." Time and space are the place of ongoing creation. Ernest Becker wrote his powerful book, *The Denial of Death,* when he himself was experiencing the voracious grip of cancer. The call he heard was in the very face of a world in which every living thing is food for something else, as each of us helps death by turning this world into a smelly dung heap. His

149

call is for faith as an heroic "nevertheless," gambling steadfastly in the face of nonbeing itself. He perseveres so that in the final moment of life one might drop one's life as gift into the cauldron of the Abyss. Somehow, for me, this has a ring not distant from the options that the Church embraces as inheritance, especially making contact with cosmic time.

In classical theology, the pattern for one's "life time" is called the *ordo salutus*—the order or pattern of salvation. Wesley, for example, drawing his *ordo* from his own experience, saw it beginning with the human condition as determined by sin, both original and personal. Yet even in this state, God offers "prevenient grace," making it possible for the self to repent. As a consequence, justification by faith is given as a gift, in which Christ's atonement on the cross is appropriated for the self, in the present. The result is a "new birth," making it possible to respond to the gracious invitations of Christ to grow in grace. This is the ongoing stage called sanctification. The goal of such spiritual growth is "Christian perfection," best understood as a conversion of motive. While one will make mistakes, a person in this state will not willfully intend harm to anyone. Whether this state can be attained in this life is not clear for Wesley. What is clear is that glorification awaits us as the final goal of heaven, disclosing that for which we have been striving for a lifetime. Whichever direction the Christian moves in understanding one's "life journey," at its heart is the question of *time*—of how past, present, and future relate.

8. Jubilee and Sabbath Time

The number *seven* has been extremely important in Hebrew Scripture as a way in which time is sacred. The Sabbath that comes every seventh day renders days into weeks. In Genesis, God's initial work of creation is portrayed as being completed in six days, and on the seventh God "rested." A better term is that God "enjoyed" the creation, in whole and in every part. Seven applied to "yearly time" resulted in each field being left fallow every seventh year, to "rest" in order that it might be restored. This idea of the seventh year is still practiced in academic institutions, where a "sabbatical" is given to each professor every seventh year, so that one can be restored through rest and research and begin again with an imagination that has regained a pregnancy for teaching.

Seven times seven, in turn, results in the sabbatical of the fiftieth year—called the "Jubilee Year." Here the whole image of rest and imaginative restoration is rendered economic. Debts are to be forgiven, and confiscated or even purchased land is returned to the original owners. In other words, justice is restored to the social order by eliminating economic inequality, thereby creating a level playing field on which to begin again. In Jesus Christ, God came into human history so that history might enter into God's time. The fullness of time *is* eternity, and thus to sanctify time is to render time a dimension of God.

With the beginning of the Third Millennium, there has been much talk about this chronological transition being a time of "Jubilee." Some extreme views have been connected to this idea, such as an apocalyptic view in which the end of time will occur in terrifying fashion. The Hebraic understanding is more optimistic. The condition out of which this idea of Jubilee arose was the certainty that unless time is "corrected" according to a pattern, time becomes destructive. So it is with people. Persons who boast of never taking a day off, or never taking a vacation, are persons who fail to understand Jubilee or Sabbath time as necessary for everyone and everything. Without it, a person damages friendships and blights one's family.

We can have something of the jubilee idea in realizing that "inheritance" implies contrasting beginning places for different children. It is to realize as well that any arrangement of "separate but equal" makes for inequality. Thus an example of Jubilee might be "Headstart:" permitting disadvantaged children to reach the first step of schooling on more equal terms. Some are advocating a Jubilee for Third World countries. This would mean reducing or eliminating the debts "owed" the United States, for efforts to pay them are becoming a crushing burden, especially on the poor. A Christian premise is that the Creator God gives the earth to all. Thereby, flying in the fact of secularism, the Church must declare that the riches of Creation are sacred, in which being stewards of the earth takes primacy over the competitive dynamic of "ownership." The Creation is to be pictured as contained in an Eucharistic vessel, distributed for the common good of the whole of humanity.

Dostoyevsky wisely perceived that a society should be evaluated not by how it deals with its rich, but how it deals with its criminals. So posed, the truth is that in American society we are witnessing a severe change in attitude toward those accused of crime. Although the name "reformatory" still remains, the penal system in this country is no longer based on *any* sense of restorative justice, but has become blatantly intended for punishment. The most recent expression of this is the cutting off of all funds previously available for furthering a prisoner's education. Even though the great majority of prisoners are illiterate, any effort to change this has been rejected as "coddling." The apparent logic is to make prison conditions so severe that "ex-cons" will be frightened from committing crime again. The opposite is occurring, as prisoners learn from each other how to be more accomplished criminals, motivated not by "repentance" but by increased anger sufficient to overcome any threat. "Three strikes and you're out" expresses clearly that the goal of prisons is not rehabilitation but our own brand of "ethnic cleansing."

Pope John Paul II recently declared that every new social condition requires a "systematic reformulation of the Church's entire social doctrine." In another observation, he wisely declared that the more the West is becoming estranged from its Christian roots, the more it is an urgent mission territory. It is very strange that our country, supposedly pledged to freedom and justice for all, should be in such desperate straits that the strong prophetic voice of the Church is needed even to plant the seeds of Jubilee in us. *Forgiveness is the clue for sacralizing time.* Pope John Paul II wisely declared that Jubilee means that "Christ is the Lord of time; he is its beginning and its end. Every year, every day, and every moment are embraced by his Incarnation and Resurrection."[8]

CHAPTER SIX

Time as Lived

"Yours is the day, yours also the night . . . . You have fixed all the bounds of the earth." (Ps. 74:16-17)
"Seven times a day I praise you." (Ps. 119:164)
"Let my prayer be counted as incense before you,
and the lifting up of my hands as an evening sacrifice." (Ps. 141:2)

1. Yearly Time—The Liturgical Seasons

The kinds of time we have developed so far in terms of liturgy coincide well with *nature,* which supplies sacred space for sacred time in a pregnant interplay. The same holds true for "yearly time." The crispness of fall, the wind fleecing the red-orange leaves from the trees, the fields yellow with harvest—one stands watching these in the twilight, tasting with delight the crisp juiciness of a freshly picked apple. The heavens migrate toward a full harvest moon, and the birds follow in kind. Time makes its presence known as the days relentlessly shorten, fall cut off prematurely with the surprise of the quiet and gentle first snowfall. The frozen ice makes zinging noises as it cracks, anticipating the spring demise. Always welcomed, crocuses appear in melting snow, as all of nature stirs in restlessness. Spring breaks forth in noisy array, the incredible freshness as shades of green. Winter does not go easily away, yet venturesome birds sing the song of resurrection in the fresh mornings.

154

Built upon nature's liturgical rhythms is "Yearly Time," as named and lived by the Church. This nature cycle gives rise to the two major seasons of the Christian year: Christmas and Easter. Advent and Lent are in the subjunctive mood; Christmas and Easter address us in the indicative mood; Epiphany and Pentecost in the imperative. Redemption itself comes always in that order. There are six seasons in all, and each season except Advent begins and ends with a special day. Advent and Lent celebrate "God *with* us." Christmas and Easter celebrate "God *for* us." And Epiphany and Pentecost celebrate "God *in* us." Since Christ's entire life is a parable—*the* parable—all these markings of time are necessary to do justice to the whole. The Christ event is the center of our lives and of all time and space—as the center, key, and purpose of the whole.

The temporal cycle of the Christian year was complete by the fourth century, with fixed dates for the honoring of the saints being developed subsequently. Christmas and Easter are the centerpieces of the two segments of the Church year. It is ironic, however, that these two times of great joy are the times when most suicides occur. I am convinced that the reason for this is that *time present,* which is intended to be *future-oriented,* becomes smothered by images of *time past.* The older we become, the more the singing of "Silent Night" on Christmas Eve brings tears, as we remember some time long ago—when we were a child singing while holding the hand of a parent now dead, or having Christmases with children now far away, or being at special places long gone. Our eyes can become myopic through a cataract of the past, and the central yearly events become distorted by feelings of sadness, regret, absence, guilt, rejection, loneliness, and abandonment.

155

The central events of the Christian faith, however, do not simply call for a remembrance of things past. In fact, it is wrong to regard God's revelation in Jesus Christ simply as what God did for thirty-two years and then returned to how and where and who God was before the Incarnation. That event is no aberration of the way God works at other times. Rather, in regarding Jesus Christ as *the* revelation of "very God of very God," *these events become the definitive disclosure of God's inmost nature, always. In Jesus Christ we have the definitive disclosure of what God is doing everywhere, in every aspect of the cosmos, in every dimension of time.*

Therefore Christian spirituality in dealing with yearly time entails, once again, a process of formation by which one literally sees all things differently. This formation makes it possible to live the present in light of the past and in anticipation of the future. This requires an emptying of the "habits of the heart" with which present society equips us. None of us ever sees anything nakedly. What one sees depends on the "set of eyes" through which one looks. For example, while as humans we negotiate well in the world of solid objects and hard surfaces, some scientists operate on a micro-level of perception where, in spite of all appearances, everything is composed of invisible whirling atoms reducible to energy. On the other end, astronomers function on a macro-level, wherein twinkling stars, almost within the reach of poets, relate vaguely in distances measured inconceivably as billions of light years.

The Christian understands, then, what Augustine meant in saying that "I believe in order to understand." Belief provides God's vantage-point. Thus if one regards major events such as Christmas not as ways of seeing but as the recalling of things past, one is condemned to live by facing backwards, trying to pump new life into an old story—by adding frills such as the fable of "The Other Wise Man," or adding a boy with a drum to the stable scene, or having Rudolf fly the friendly skies. Thus such events as Christmas or Easter are not really conclusions drawn from the way the Christian sees things, but the contrary. They are faith's presupposition without which we cannot truly see at all. As presupposition, then, the church year emerges as a vision so compelling that the presupposition, in turn, becomes almost self-evident for the Christian. Even God is to be perceived through eyes shaped by the contours of the divine event called Jesus-as-the-Christ.

Probably the type of time most familiar to Christians is the one to which we now turn—yearly time as the "church year." Instead of seeing the simple chronology of one year following another, the Church recognizes a primal rhythm upon which all yearly time rests. What follows is a sketch of that arrangement:

YEAR TIME

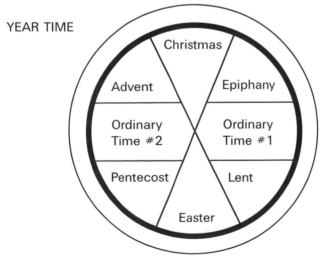

As the diagram suggests, the church year has two segments of three divisions each. Each segment is followed with two long periods of "ordinary time," together totaling thirty-three or thirty-four weeks, occurring from Epiphany to Ash Wednesday, and from Pentecost to Advent. The rhythm of each triad is that of Promise / Fulfillment / Response. The center point for the first triad, then, is Incarnation (Christmas); the second center point is Resurrection (Easter). Their intersection forms the center point where Christians stand to see. Looking through the Advent aperture as promise, one is touched by the historical sweep of human yearning for completion. Looking through the Lenten aperture, we experience deep remorse over where such yearnings have taken us. Therefore the first triad of promise, fulfillment, response is concretized as Advent, Christmas, Epiphany. The second triad is concretized as Lent, Easter, Pentecost. An inclusive expression of these threefold movements is this:

1. Restlessness, yearning, preparation, promise, contrition
2. Reception, answer, fulfillment, being
3. Response, call, sending, resolution, living the vision

Christmas as incarnation is special in that it restores the eyes of innocence that once characterized Eden—as if seeing life through the fresh and sparkling eyes of a child. Easter, as resurrection, entails a different vantage—where in another garden Mary Magdalene's world-weary eyes gaze longingly at the "stranger." Here resurrection becomes incarnation restored as promise. The response of Epiphany is to perceive life itself as mission, paralleling the

eyes of incarnation, which discern birth pangs everywhere. It is a consequence of Christmas, and Christmas
the fulfillment of Advent—as God's created intention for
the world. The Pentecostal response entails the re-promising
of incarnation, viewed as the consummation of a new
heaven and a new earth. Pentecost is a consequence of
Easter, Easter the fulfillment of Lent—as God's redeeming
response to the world's blindness.

As preparation for the first period of "ordinary time,"
Christian living entails action evoked by seeing through
the reflexive lens of the triad of Advent / Christmas /
Epiphany. These seasons help us rehearse incarnational
seeing. As a result, one can perceive the intersection of
divine and human in everything: a cup of coffee on a frosty
morning, the first mockingbird in spring, autumn sunlight
through painted leaves, city lights during a night flight, a
deer clearing a meadow fence on a snowy morning. These
are innocent moments when time stops, as if beholding
the first star when creation danced into being at God's
invitation. A newspaper's Christmas cartoon that illustrates
this stance well is one in which gift-laden adults trudge
wearily through the snow. In the middle of them stands a
child, gleefully catching snowflakes with her tongue.
"Unless you change and become like children . . . " (Matt.
18:3). But in the faces of the adults, life has become like
salt "that has lost its taste"; it is an interminable sameness,
"no longer good for anything, . . . [except to be] thrown
out and trodden under foot" (Matt. 5:13). To be reborn
with Christmas eyes is to be blessed, if only for moments
at a time, with the wide-open, innocent eyes of a child.

Just as the Holy Spirit ravished Mary with the pregnancy
known as Jesus, so the Spirit continues at Pentecost as an

159

incarnation within each of us. "Do you not know that you are God's temple and that God's Spirit dwells in you?" (1 Cor. 3:16). This ongoing incarnation within us enables us to perceive God's ongoing incarnation without as Christmas gifts of the Incarnate Spirit. Even the secular world is forced to recognize this Christmas specialness, although they call it Christmas "magic": the sparkle of tinsel, the smell of turkey, the sight of the first snow, and the sounds of children. Without such "magic," everything is reduced to being a means to some self-serving end. Instead of seeing faith as a means to keep the family together or to get to heaven, we need Christmas eyes so we can perceive the invitation to experience life itself as sheer gift, as an absolute delight. God revels in being human from within. For the Christian, "real presence" becomes visible in every birth, as countless galaxies are ablaze with glory, and all the "hills are alive with the sound of music, with songs they have sung for a thousand years."

In this first triad, Advent is an expectant longing, in which God's original promise of the Messiah has become an anticipation of the one who has promised to *come again*. The Lenten preparation through promise is somewhat different, much as Creation relates to Re-creation, or Redemption. "Though your sins are like scarlet, they shall be as white as snow" (Is. 1:18 RSV). Lent is not the eager anticipation of a joyous birth, but the anxieties of participating in a bloody extermination, not even daring to hope in rebirth. Lent is not the time to anticipate gifts. It is the time of anticipating Jesus' hanging on the cross as the pathos of a world cracked and contaminated, and a people involved in the arrogance of "ethnic cleansing," or the self-deception of holding to "separate but equal" policies, whether in terms of gender, class, race, sexuality, or intelligence. Is it too much to ask that Christians stop killing each other? The picture that speaks to me of a Lenten-strewn Easter is of an African American child, walking with eager smile across a glass-strewn ghetto lot, proudly carrying an Easter lily almost as large as he is. The hope is not "because" but "nevertheless."

We have lost our innocence. We know better than to walk the city streets after dark—and so we ache for Eden, where it is safe enough to walk with God "in the garden in the cool of the day." Sadly, there is no way back. To think there is makes such hope as thin as Santa is imaginary. The Christmas tree browns; the balls fall; the toys break. No Christmas lasts for long. It's particularly dislocating that the culture *stops* celebrating Christmas just when the Church is *starting* its Christmas season celebrations. Consequently the divine promise that makes all things new is relinquished unless we can hyphenate Christmas and Easter—incarnation *as* resurrection. The Incarnate God experiences all things from within, and nothing of value is ever lost, for all things of worth are redeemed when they are resurrected in the divine memory. Therefore, Christmas hope, rooted in the past, looks forward to the future; it looks through the desert of lost innocence into the Promised Land of redeemed childlikeness. When the One who came as a child is seen through Lenten eyes as the crucified Lord, the Resurrection in turn promises a re-creation arrayed as if it is a Christmas tree.

The Christian faith, as disclosed so poignantly through the eyes of the church year, really trusts that the God who makes promises also keeps them. From Christmas joy through broken New Year's resolutions, from Lenten repentance to the Easter promise of victory over death, from tattered anticipations to restored expectations—on and on goes the redeeming cycle of the church year. Or again, Christmas is the name for what Easter eyes can see, purged by Good Friday so they can perceive the yearning for, and the promise of, incarnation everywhere. Risking the promise, over and over again, brings the "second naïveté," as Paul Ricoeur calls it. And ordinary time is transformed by being seen through restored seeing.

Christmas hiddenness occurs in being revealed; Easter is a revealing that occurs in being hidden. Easter eyes are not possible if one's Christmas hopes have not been dashed. And through Lent we experience disillusionment, doubt, despair, and death as a sacrament of defeat. The sin that tempts us most during ordinary time is to take things for granted. Only the threat of losing everything (crucifixion) can open our eyes to see things freshly as gift (incarnation), as if for the first time (resurrection). With this transformation, hiddenness becomes a delight. A flower hinted at through its fragrance, a bird seen only by its call, a midnight snow sensed by the silence—these are the Holy Spirit teasing us into an Advent yearning, luring, hoping, hinting, anticipating the Easter promise for all that is.

Trust is difficult, but it is the foundation of everything. One dares trust only an Incarnate God who has been crucified. Only trust the hope of a Christian who has gone through the valley of the shadow of death. Only trust the yearnings of those who include every blade of grass and every speck of dust in their dream. Only trust a cosmos whose adorning is choreographed by the One concerned to "wipe away every tear from [our] eyes [so that] death will be no more" (Rev. 21:4). Our Christmas-Easter toast is

162

wine drunk from a chalice—trusting Christmas as God being eternally born, and Easter as Christ being resurrected everywhere. Ours is the task of gambling on the abundant hints we receive, followed by faithful guesses. Hints are "the miraculous works of the fingers of God, and the morning stars that always so merrily stand before the face of God, ministering to Him."[1] But the greatest wager is that these eyes of faith—of incarnation / resurrection—are the eyes through which God also sees the world.

In the end, these two triads of promise, fulfillment, and response are not to be understood simply as special times—as if they are inserted to break up the monotony of ordinary time. Rather, *they are the dress rehearsals so that one can live the ordinary in an extraordinary way.* Life presents us with two huge and contrasting options. One can guzzle life to the dregs by clutching everything as "Christmas gifts for *me*." Or one may make of one's life a Christmas gift for God, thankfully returned to God "with much interest."[2] And lest one forget the profound meaning of ordinary time, there are feast days, as festivals scattered like manna across the days of ordinary time. These mostly celebrate the martyrdom and/or faithfulness of the saints who preceded us, so we may model our days on theirs, in sacred remembrance. On several of the major feast days, I sent my students out into the city to see what most persons did then. For those not in church, it was the mall where "feasts" are "celebrated," in buying and selling.

The psalmist proposes resolving life's enigmas with a harp. I insist that one do so by dancing to a melody. By tapping one foot restlessly before an abandoned stable, the other foot dances lithely before an empty tomb. Each of us is called to be a Christmas gift to the world—giving tantalizing glimpses of life lived outrageously at death's edge, where at Easter we give it all away in childlike delight. Everything is gift, and re-gift, and re-gift again.

ADVENT AND CHRISTMAS

Christian festivals are most often events of contrast, and thus their hope relies on promise. For example, Christmas as the Feast of Lights occurs in the Northern Hemisphere when the world is covered with the longest darkness, with days of shortest light. Thus the center of Advent is our longing, our restlessness, our search and pilgrimage for light as hope. The Roman Catholic *Ordo* puts this well: "While the powers of darkness speak ever more loudly of doom and destruction, Christians celebrate with dauntless hope manifestations of glory which reduce to nothing the arms and weapons of the mighty."[3] Ironically, the victory seems an impossible one, for the savior story is of a rustic manger and poor itinerant parents. Yet it is at that manger as "sacred space" that earth and heaven meet. And kneeling there, one senses the divine as the Mystery whose meaning we still seek. A reliable sign for me is that when they are preparing for Christmas, monks become more playful.

THE CHRISTMAS SEASON

This season extends from evening prayer on Christmas through the Baptism of Christ (the Sunday after January 6). Epiphany (January 6) is the beginning of our response as mission, with the Magnificat serving as Christianity's social creed. Since feasts are practices that help one to live more meaningfully in ordinary time, Christmas is a rehearsal for receiving every thing and every time as gift-wrapped. In fact, it is the celebration of God being born in each soul.

LENT AND ASH WEDNESDAY

Lent, meaning "spring," is the forty days after Ash Wednesday, not counting Sundays. Both in Lent and Advent, as in the rest of the year, every Sunday is the celebration of the Resurrection as Christ, and thus it has priority over every other feast or observance. Interestingly, there are two distinct Ash Wednesday blessings, giving to Lent alternative flavors. The choice is the prerogative of the minister. The one most known is "Remember that you are dust, and to dust you shall return." Here one has forty days in which to meditate upon the shortness of our lives and our fragility as dust. In effect, we are to become ready for Easter as the victory over death. We recall the Passover, when God kept the angel of death from killing the Jews. The second alternative blessing is "Turn away from sin and be faithful to the gospel." Lent so begun becomes a time of repentance, suffering with Christ through Good Friday, where the supreme suffering on Good Friday is declared by Easter to be sufficient for forgiveness.

Even the meaning of "giving up" something for Lent has a different import in the light of each of these blessings. For the first, the significance is that of emptying through fasting, much as hunger is a vehicle for experiencing one's fragility. The most powerful image is that of Passover as respite from death. For those living the second blessing, the key is sacrifice, participating in some small way with

Christ's suffering. The most powerful image here is that of the paschal lamb, slain at Passover, evoking the image of the scapegoat sent out into the wilderness with the sins of the people on his "shoulders." Lent, in each case, is to be "endured" as hope, promise, and anticipation, but likewise as being too good to be true.

Lent is the time in which Jesus prepared for his own death, and so Lent is about our death. Above all, the death that counts is the death of our finite supports so that we stand nakedly before God, the only true support. In Lent, one dares to explore the deepest meanings and the mystery of human life. And the promise of resurrection extends to all things in all worlds—alleluia!—with the eight days following Easter intense with fulfilled happiness.

PALM SUNDAY OR PASSION SUNDAY

Palm Sunday is the day of the joyous messianic entrance—but once we have entered, we greet the day with pensive eyes, for at the center of the liturgy stands the entire Holy Week story as the Gospel lesson. In the Roman Catholic Church the people stand for the whole reading, with parts often taken by various members and the congregation taking the role of the "crowd." It is as if one suddenly is condemned by the palm branches in one's hand, for the Messiah that we are acclaiming is the one we will help destroy in less than a week. The clergy wear red vestments, giving this Sunday the tension of celebration and betrayal, gift and loss, life and death. Every Sunday, from that point on, will have a procession of priest or pastor as a remembrance of this Palm Sunday procession.

166

THE TRIDUUM

The *Triduum,* which we will explore in depth later, are the three days that are for the Christian the *primal* event of all time and space. It is the Time of times, beginning with the Lord's Supper on Thursday evening, ending at Vespers on Easter Sunday.

Maundy Thursday. This service differs greatly for Protestants and Catholics. For Protestants, the mood of Maundy Thursday is solemn, often ending with a Tenebrae ("darkness"). This is a visual act with twelve purple candles and a white one in the middle. The Scripture is read, and as each disciple abandons Jesus, a candle is snuffed out. When only the Christ candle is left, in the semidarkness the worshipers stumble in finding their way to the door. In some services even the white candle is extinguished, with a startling gong or the slamming shut of a large Bible.

For Protestants, the primary Maundy Thursday event, then, is the *Last* Supper, and the service has the mood of farewell. For the Catholic, the preferred name is the *Lord's* Supper, where Jesus promised that he would not leave us fatherless, as orphans. Not only would he send the Holy Spirit as Comforter, but also in this very supper he promised that from then on, at the breaking of bread as Eucharist, Christ would be Present. This Presence is "Real," in a manner fully reminiscent of his presence with them on that Thursday. This is not a time for sadness. Rather, the emphasis is upon the Eucharist at which Jesus himself will be present, again and again. Although in a deep sense this is the end; it is also the beginning. The sadness comes afterwards, when one by one we are identified as negative answers to Jesus' question: "So could you not stay awake with me one hour?" (Matt. 26:40). The answer is "No."

Privately the altar is stripped; crosses are often covered with red or purple; all candles and lamps are extinguished; the holy water is removed from all fonts and, in some churches, the fonts are filled with sand. This scarcity stands in heavy contrast with the Easter Vigil when they are refilled, and water flows abundantly through the whole service. The tank for baptism by immersion remains in the church throughout the fifty days of the Easter season, and parishioners are encouraged to wash their hands and face in it, even splashing playfully in the water, during the time of confession and forgiveness at each Eucharist.

Good Friday. This sacred day may be observed with a service based on the seven last words of Jesus, or with a Tenebrae. For Catholics the Celebration of the Lord's Passion is generally at 3:00 PM. There are three parts to the service: the Word heard and proclaimed, veneration of the cross with a kiss, and communion of "leftovers" from the Maundy Thursday Mass. All of "Christ's Body" is consumed at this service, so that at its conclusion the "pantry" is bare. We are shut off from the spiritual nurture of Christ's Body and Blood—for Christ is dead, and so we are spiritual orphans. After the service everything is removed. Even the hollow sounds of the church creak of emptiness.

Holy Saturday presents us with a unique mood—a tension of emptiness with hints of anticipation. The image one might have is that of Christ in the tomb. But another image is more powerful: An early Church tradition affirms that in his death Christ descended into hell, preaching the good news and freeing all who responded to such love. A prayer by St. Bridget on her Vigil feast (July

23) is particularly powerful on this day. "And after forty days you ascended into heaven before the eyes of many witnesses, and there in heaven you gathered together in glory those you love, whom you have freed from hell."[4] Another element of Holy Saturday imagery is that of the sorrowing mother at the foot of the cross. Stark symbols or pictures of such images may be placed in the church to evoke prayer by the faithful.

Easter Vigil is the most sacred of all Christian time. In the Roman Catholic Church it begins and ends in darkness, usually early Easter morning. In the Episcopal Church, the Easter Vigil begins in early morning darkness and ends in the blazing sun of a new day. There are seven Old Testament readings and two from the New Testament; the stories reveal the progression of time from the Genesis story of creation to the resurrection of Jesus Christ. Although some of the readings can be skipped, appropriately the story of the Passover must be read, for this very night Christ becomes our Passover. "Alleluia" is neither said nor sung during Lent, for preparation for death is not something one would choose to celebrate. Thus shouts and songs of "Alleluia" are the way the congregation responds to the declaration during the Vigil of Christ's victory over death. The liturgy for the entire Easter Season is peppered with Alleluias, and during the first octave of Easter (eight days), the alleluias are always doubled. "Alleluia, Alleluia."

A central feature of the Easter Vigil is the Baptism of new Christians. Interestingly, Baptism for Protestants means being washed, cleansed, and made new; thus it appropriately may be done at various times. For Catholics, on the other hand, Baptism is basically about going down with Christ into his death, and one is immersed three times to symbolize the three days in the tomb. Then the person is raised up from the water with the resurrected Christ in all his glory. Thus Baptism is particularly appropriate at the Vigil. The joy comes because one's own death has just occurred, and thus death is no longer to be feared. It is behind us. The congregation welcomes the new Christians in the presence of the endless line of saints, called forth by name.

Food may be blessed after the Vigil, or after the Easter morning Eucharist, just as Jesus ate with his disciples on the morning of his Resurrection. Since all fasting is behind, even when the congregation prays, it is done standing, not kneeling. With an intermingling of spiritual and physical food, the fast of Lent is broken, and the church is radiant with flowers and joy. What Sunday is to each week, the Easter Season is to the liturgical year, each, interestingly, about a seventh of their respective times.

The significance of time in these events is rich. In one sense, they are the remembrance of things past, for the Church insists that Christ's sacrifice happened once and for all. And yet, in a deep sense, what happened as a past event is meant for the present in the light of the future. Christmas and Easter in their deepest senses are eternal acts, indeed, cosmic acts—celebrated as the Mystery of timeless events immersed in time. In the Triduum, as we shall see, the imagery tumbles forth in rich array, so that the imagination can see these three days as the wedding of the Lamb, and the Easter season a celebration of the divine honeymoon. Traditionally during these days the new communicants received special catechesis or instruction about the Sacraments.

170

EASTER SEASON

The Easter season is marked by fifty days of festive joy. The time from Easter to Pentecost is celebrated as one "great Sunday," as a never-ending day. Easter season is the time to embrace in one resounding "yes" the length and breadth, the heights and depths, of all creation, with everything marinated in hope. This is the "yes" one can hear in the play of light and shadow in Mozart's later piano concerti. Or more simply, one can hear it "in the delighted squeals of a child as its face is licked by the moist tongue and hot breath of a new puppy."[5] The huge Paschal Candle, lit as a preface for the Easter Vigil, not only provides light for the procession, but remains near both altar and lectern, as a symbol of the presence of the risen Christ in the midst of his people. It is lit for all services until the Vespers of Pentecost, for Jesus promised never to abandon us or leave us alone. So the candle of his presence remains until the Holy Spirit descends as the continuation of his incarnation in us.

The Easter season is a traditional time to have one's home blessed, as an invitation to the Spirit to make his abode with us. With the ending of Pentecost, the recessional includes the Easter candle. The Easter season is over. Ordinary time begins.

ASCENSION

Carl Braaten contrasts time as "eschatological" (extrapolating from the present to the future) and time as "apocalyptic" (interpolating from the future to the present). The Latin derivative for the first is *futurum*, meaning actualizing potentialities. The second is rooted in *Adventus*, meaning the coming of what is radically new. He affirms that the second term is the Christian understanding. The Resurrection is utterly new, in no way predictable in the light of the ghastly Crucifixion. Thus what is new is not some affirmation of immortality of the soul. As St. Leo put it, the ascended Christ is still the wounded Christ, and so is the One who will return. Thus though we are human, so is Jesus, and through him we share in his divinity. The Ascension is the ongoing promise that through Jesus Christ, the work of our hands and of our minds and our deepest feelings are being taken up into the becoming of God. Jesus now lives in the immensity of God, and has promised that we, too, can add to God's immensity.

PENTECOST

It we take an expansive understanding of Pentecost, we understand that the Spirit is incarnated not only in our inner essence as our soul, but also operates in everything that lives. Thus the season of Pentecost calls us, as the *Ordo* says, to learn how to say "Yes" in a culture that wants to keep saying "No." Like Passover, Pentecost originated as a Jewish feast. Leviticus 23:16 indicates it as the day after the seventh Sabbath, namely fifty days. It is the time in which Jews offered God the best grain from the harvest. It is also a time of remembrance for the law given to Moses on Mount Sinai. Paul contrasts this gift of the law with God's gift of the Holy Spirit (2 Cor. 3:7-8). Pentecost is the *birthday of the Church*—for the Holy Spirit who came upon Mary, resulting in the Incarnation, is now the Spirit who can invade our souls, making of us a temple in which the divine may dwell. Interestingly, Mary is apparently present at this second visitation of the Spirit as well. The Vigil of Pentecost is celebrated on the evening before, with prayers that Christ's promise will be forthcoming. At the Vespers of Pentecost the Easter Candle is extinguished. The Easter season is completed.

ALL SAINTS

One of the significant differences between the secular calendar and the liturgical calendar is the celebration of saints, observed on the day of their death as their entry into eternal time. Thus the Church would observe Martin Luther King Jr. Day not on his birthday, but on the date of his assassination. Often churches will have a special book where people can inscribe the names of their special dead, for whom prayers are said. A powerful moment in my ordination was when, as I lay prostrate on the floor, the congregation chanted an invitation to over thirty saints by name. The Church, far from being just the little building on the corner across from the gas station, expands to be the concrete intersection of all time and all space.

CHRIST THE KING

With the festival of "Christ the King," the church year comes to a crescendo. It is the last Sunday before Advent. Here we catch a glimpse and foretaste of the Kingdom of God, toward which all of history is moving, and for which we have been working and praying. Thomas Oden describes this feast well, suggesting how a Christian ethic emerges from it. We are to act so that our aim coincides with the inner drive of every creature toward fulfillment in the Kingdom of God. The powerful image for this feast is that of a joyous wedding feast, or a great supper—so great in fact that we are sent out into the byways to bring everyone to the feast. Oden interprets this injunction to mean that we are to go to the bars, racetracks, skid rows, to invite the poor, transients, sick, old, retarded, blind, prostitutes, and "bums"—these are the people who cannot repay. It will be a time when old enmities are settled, and African Americans will "sit down with Birmingham white people, and Nazis sit down with Jews, Communists with Capitalists, and they will all be one."[6] St. Bernard in his *On Loving God* adds to this vision. The Kingdom will be where "there is fullness without disgust, insatiable curiosity which is not restless, an eternal and endless desire which knows no lack; and lastly, that sober intoxication which does not come from drinking too much, which is no reeking of mind, but a burning for God."[7]

2. Monthly Time

I have never heard monthly time discussed or recognized in church circles. The sun and its travels determine most kinds of time. Monthly time, in contrast, is based on lunar time—a time that has been quite influential in certain cultures in the past. In part, its rediscovery has been due to the "women's movement" and makes cognizant a significant dimension of "female time."

My attention to this dimension of time was evoked by a NASA study of the emotional impact of a woman's monthly period on her ability to function in space physically and emotionally. The study concluded that indeed women had monthly cycles, which involve a high-low emotional rhythm. They should have stopped while they were ahead, but they thought in all fairness they should study men also—arguably in order to show how much more stable an all-male astronaut team would be. Unexpectedly, however, the study identified a monthly cycle for males as well. In fact men are more at a disadvantage because they have no physical signals to designate when their cycles are occurring.

The implication of *monthly time* for the Christian is that it provides a way of dealing creatively with variable moods in one's spirituality. The sudden shift of one's "emotions" can be frightening for either gender, when one is unable to account for that inversion. The first response is to become alarmed, suspecting there is something wrong with one's body. But some of us are discovering that the making of a "lunar calendar" to discern the length of one's cycle can be relevant for one's spirituality; the cycle may be as short as twenty-five days and for others over a month. While there will be some variations, the basic rhythm is constant. Then, instead of being hit broadside emotionally, one can chart the days when life will tend toward the ecstatic, even if the particular events occurring on those days are far from conducive to joy. And there are days in which one is so sad that even the best of events can hardly break open the "negative" emotion.

By using this type of calendar, both women and men can plan so that the cycle becomes a "carrier" for Christian living. I can still remember the first time that I discovered all this. On the days of "depression" my reading of the Crucifixion of Christ became powerfully alive. And nothing can be much better than reading about the Resurrection, Ascension, and Kingdom when one's cycle is at its highest point. Both tears and giggles make for a significant rhythm in one's spiritual life.

3. Weekly Time

During the Middle Ages, when literacy was low, the Church used the arts as instruments of communication. Stained-glass windows, for example, served as one's catechism. Memorization readily implanted the poetry of faith in one's mind. I am amazed that even uneducated monks memorized all 150 psalms in latin so they could sing them while working in the fields. Likewise people acted out the biblical stories, using an xintermingling of drama and liturgy. The earliest Christians continued to worship in the Jewish Temple and in synagogues, as Jesus had done. They supplemented this worship with a daily gathering in the upper room, eating a sacred meal in remembrance of the Lord's Supper. As the number of believers grew, they observed the Eucharist every Sunday morning, for that was the day when Christ rose from the dead. As this sort of association fell into place, since Sunday was a "little Easter" observed weekly in celebration of the Resurrection, it easily followed that every Friday might be observed as a "little Good Friday." And as discipline called for a fast preceding the weekly Eucharist, a disciplined time of self-denial came to characterize Friday—symbolized by eating fish rather than meat. Yearly, Ash Wednesday and Good Friday became times of serious fasting, in which the main meal on these days, at least for monks, is water and bread. The only liberalism I can detect is the choice of whether one drinks hot or cold water.

Perhaps the most misunderstood part of observing weekly time regards the Sabbath. The Sabbath observance followed the Genesis story that after six days of strenuous creating, "God rested." In the family of my rearing the

Sabbath was taken negatively. One must *refrain* from almost everything. I could not play. There was no cooking. No one could buy a newspaper. One just had to go to Church, and be quiet, very quiet. I was on the edge of losing all religion when the pastor once said, "Heaven will be like a perpetual Sunday." Strangely, it was the monastery that showed me otherwise—that the negative is for the sake of the positive. God *refrained* from work in order to be able to *enjoy* the incredible beauty of the Milky Way that he had thrown and the delicate petals of the roses he grew. Supposedly he also took time to laugh with the giraffe, for it was not one of his better works of art. Sunday is like being given a total day off, not to work but to enjoy, to play.

The Sabbath is not only a particular day of the week, it is also a mode of living. Unfortunately the mechanical clock attempts to govern our whole lives. In our economic system, time is money, pressuring us to hurry production so we can eke out as much profit as possible. It follows that what is of value is to produce things or services that can be sold. Meanwhile, guilt is bred into us from birth to guarantee that we won't "waste time." As a result, in many ways, work has become our religion, and consumption has become our idol. Therefore it is extremely difficult for Americans to *play*. It should be no surprise, then, that even in "play," society makes sure that one will be involved in buying and selling. Whether it is an increasingly expensive set of golf clubs, or the incredibly expensive "right" pair of sneakers, we can't play without the necessary equipment.

Furthermore, play is usually made into the means for something else. The usual justification for "play" is that it has "value" because it helps a person plunge back more

intensely into one's work. The most valued "play" is a
ticket to watch others play, especially from the fifty-yard
line. And the kind of games we are most inclined to watch
are characterized by a savage competitiveness that simply
continues the "no-play" culture of our daily world. I am
ashamed to acknowledge that for a long period after my
children left home, I had neither been to a zoo nor flown
a kite. The children had been my permission to be playful.

I am a Mickey Mouse fan, complete with the ears. He
and I can "be silly" together, especially with the grandchildren. I have a theory. When I went to Mickey's "Magic
Kingdom" there were an incredible number of older persons
wheeling tiny children in carriages. There was no way that
these infants had any clue where they were, or even cared,
as long as the bottle was near by. The grandchildren were
simply the excuse for the grandparents to eat cotton candy
again.

What Christians truly need is a renewal of the meaning
of Sabbath, complete with God as the model. The Creator
of heaven and earth is described by the Scripture as the
original and best of players. Creative activity is playful,
and creative people rarely feel that what they do is work.
They have a notion that their creativity and all that they
create are divine gifts. Thus the Christian's response is a
thankful one, giving meaning to weekly Masses that are
called "Eucharist," a word that means "thankfulness."

Tilden Edwards reminds us of the Christian tradition
that holds that on the Sabbath there is not even suffering
in hell.[8] In fact, St. Bernard advocated sex on Sunday as a
sacred rite. The Sabbath is a time of joy, no matter where
one might be. It is like living without a "program," tithing
one's time as one does one's possessions. This makes the

Sabbath qualitatively different from any other time. Chesterton called it "wasting time with God." Augustine called it "sanctified leisure" and "holy longing." Other names are "grave merriment" or "holy play." Sabbath is a matter of catching one's breath—God's breath, breathed into us as the Holy Spirit. Even Calvin affirmed recreation on the Sabbath; he favored bowling.

This understanding makes the line between play and work almost invisible. The difference is one of attitude. At times as a professor I found it strange that I was being paid for doing what I love to do. Jesus said, "Come to me, all you that are weary and are carrying heavy burdens, and I will give you rest." But immediately thereafter he adds, "Take my yoke upon you . . . and you will find rest for your souls" (Matt. 11:28, 29). To "do" out of love is play; it is doing for the sheer joy of it. Nothing is work, suggests St. Bernard, when we know God as the "lovable Lover." Early theologians referred to Sunday as the eighth day of creation, for this way of living was the goal of all that goes before. Such a view contrasts greatly with the way our society approaches our "work week." Few there are whose labor is intrinsic. For most persons, work is instrumental: That is, they make money through work that really feels like work so as to have money for enjoying life on days off or on vacations. In contrast, my oldest daughter is a photo-journalist in Idaho. Being an outdoor enthusiast, she finds her life amazing, that she gets paid for taking pictures of mountain climbing, kayaking, and sports—everything she would want to do on days off anyhow! Oden wisely notes that Sundays, like sacraments, are at the same time points of arrival and of departure, igniting the "fabric of Christian living" as a pilgrimage toward the fullness of the Kingdom.

Although my family was hardly conscious of the theological origins of our Saturday evening "liturgy," I understand it now. The big round galvanized tub, hanging outside by the back door, was brought inside. Hot water was kept boiling on the coal stove, and we always argued as to who got the first bath. We washed in each other's water, adding hot water as needed. Then we were given fresh underwear, and fell asleep on clean sheets. By morning my freshly starched shirt would be hanging at the post of my bed. Why? We dressed in our "Sunday best," for at church we were to meet the risen Lord. This same "liturgy" occurred on Easter, when it was imperative that we have something new, even if we could afford only a new bright tie.

The little coal-mining town where I was born had a practice that probably was widespread. I remember it from a ditty my mother sang, which went something like this: "Monday wash day, Tuesday ironing . . . ." I don't remember all the words, but each day of the week had its own function. I recall one Monday when the village water system broke. Would my mother shift washing to Tuesday when the pipes were repaired? Of course not, for washing is to be done on Monday! Some years later I lived in an intentional Christian community. We tried to model ourselves as much as possible after the early Church. After some research and experimentation, we arrived at a theological version of weekly time, paralleling my mother's secular one. It took this rhythm:

Weekly Rhythm
Monday: Creation
Tuesday: Fall
Wednesday: Exodus / Liberation

Thursday: Promised Land
Friday: Crucifixion / Ascension*
Saturday: Desert Waiting
Sunday: Resurrection

4. Daily Time

In order to provide a daily schedule of prayer times for the clergy, the Roman Breviary was written in 1568, bringing into uniformity other efforts. This breviary was used until 1970 when Vatican II established a new one, designed for use by laity as well. Maas underscores its importance by stating that the Christian's foundation of the breviary and the Eucharist has a dual objective. The breviary is known also as the Liturgy of the Hours, the Daily Office, or the *Opus Dei* (the Work of God). Its basic purpose is the sanctification of time. Presently seven "services" of worship each day parallels the Hebraic tradition, referred to in Psalm 119:164: "Seven times a day I praise you." Kathleen Morris whimsically likens these daily offices to the function of a service station.

The origin of the Daily Office has its foundation in the sixth century BC. During Israel's exile in the Babylonian Captivity, with their Temple in ruins, the Jews intensely needed to keep their identity by remembering their past. Sometimes such observances were done alone, at other times they were corporate. They used a rhythm of reading, reflecting, and giving thanks. Cyprian indicated that in his time (third century AD), the Church observed what he called the "sacrament of the Trinity:" reciting the Lord's Prayer three times a day. Others prayed at specific times.

At 9 AM, Christians recalled Christ's being nailed to the cross. At noon, darkness came over the land, and at 3 PM, Christ died for us.

This basic remembrance expanded to include a prayer before sleep. Some Christians interrupted their sleep for prayer at midnight. These dark times came to be regarded as particularly holy. This is the time when everything, living creatures and plants, stars and waters, are hushed for a brief time to praise their God. Following the Hebraic observance of beginning each day at sunset, the church began to have *Vigils* as a service during the night before a major feast day. This practice is still observed, as with Midnight Mass before Christmas, and the Easter Vigil in the darkness of Easter. In time, Vigils gave birth to two additional offices of *Vespers* and *Lauds*. Hippolytus in 236 indicated that this practice was already in use. Vigils (or Matins) came to have three segments, reflecting the Trinity. For balance, they had a corresponding daytime of *Terce, Sext,* and *None. Prime* developed as a time for consecrating the monk's daily labor. And the need for bedtime devotions in the monastic dormitory completed the sanctification as *Compline* ("complete"), composed of lessons, chapter of faults (confession), and the abbot's blessing. Hippolytus (170–236) tells us that he rose at midnight, washed, and prayed. By the time of St. Jerome (420), lay brothers of the monastery, farmers, and laborers prayed the psalms as they worked, having committed to memory all 150 of the Psalms in Latin! At the conclusion of chanting each psalm, the doxology was sung so as to Christianize the psalms.

These "daily hours" are really a biblical service, with an emphasis on the Psalter, for it was Christ's hymnbook. Without any mechanical device for "keeping time," the

Church's canonical hours, accompanied with bells, became the "clock" around which medieval life was formed. So crucial was this spiritual intersecting that the Mass could be likened to the sun around which the canonical hours circled much as we now understand the planets. The Daily Office provided a spiritual oasis every three hours and so, by recalling the Trinity, rendered daily time holy.

Each of these offices (times of worship) had a threefold division, corresponding to the three individual hours that formed each office. An effort was made to have the particular office correspond with the particular activity the monks might be doing during that time.

Monasteries have been largely responsible for creating and preserving this daily approach to time. The Trappists, known as "Cistercians of the Strict Observance," best illustrate the Church's present formation of daily time as observed by a monastery. The full day of twenty-four hours is divided by the Trinity, giving eight different periods. The accompanying diagram portrays this arrangement in terms of a clock inside a clock, indicating AM and PM. What is so important about this daily time is that the monk obeys Christ's teaching to live only *one day at a time*, without anticipating one's tomorrow, which may never occur, or being depressed over the past, which is forgiven. The monastic day begins with a bell at 3:15 AM, and at 3:30 the office of *Vigils* begins.[9]

VIGILS

Everything is still, even the birds. All of creation sleeps. The monks lose themselves in the solitude of silence. A mournful wind bends the pines. Coyotes wail, sometimes with terrifying sounds. This is the time when most persons die, for at this hour our hold on life is so fragile. One waits, as did the wise and foolish virgins, for the coming of the bridegroom as lover. Are we the wise? Or are we the foolish? It is hard to know. Over all is a shroud of holy gloom. Night is a symbol of our life on earth. The dark is liquid silence. These hours feel like having to live a Holy Saturday each day. This Vigil time is real, and not just a remembrance of a past event. In truth, we await the Second Coming, whose time we know not. This is the time in which the early Christians gathered underground in the catacombs, aware that martyrdom could be required of them at any moment. The mood is an ascetic one, of watching in readiness and anticipation.

And yet these dark hours are the ones monks find most propitious for peaceful contemplation, for pondering, even brooding. The night fast evokes a hunger for spiritual things. An office focuses the theme of each particular period. Vigils, as all other offices, is composed largely of psalms. They are all sung in a two-week period. (See Appendix 3 for this listing.) The rest of the time in this segment is spent in silent contemplation or *lectio divina* (sacred reading.)

LAUDS

At daybreak monks celebrate one of the two most important daily periods, the holy hours of sunrise (Lauds) and sunset (Vespers). *Lauds,* meaning "Praise," reflects the psalmist's action when he says: "I will awaken the dawn." This is the time of resurrection. The darkness is streaked by eastern light, as the horizon breaks the bonds of death. And with the sun, victory is proclaimed over the primeval chaos. Nature begins to stir, as harbinger of a new day. Lauds is particularly powerful if done in the open air.

Theologically we are greeting the dawning day of salvation. Bridegroom and bride embrace and kiss. We take Zechariah's place in the Holy of Holies, singing his *Benedictus*. Our chanting is a resurrection song for all of creation and the Church as her soul. Each morning is a coming, a coming, a coming. With or without us, each morning is a new creation, fashioned to a symphony of praise. And as we face fully to the east, each heartbeat becomes a special blessing, for everything is gift, everywhere. Here we learn, as one writer put it, to "expect nothing out of everything, and everything out of nothing." This is probably the most beautiful of the offices, full of colorful joy. The world stirs, as though awakened by a tender kiss. In many monasteries, Lauds merge into the Eucharist. It is particularly meaningful, for just as the sacralizing of bread and wine results in "Real Presence," so it is the near-perfect manner for celebrating the Resurrection.

PRIME

While the office of Prime is no longer corporately observed, to include it gives a better sense of the organic nature of the monastic day. Prime means "first": the first office after the resurrection. So it is with all offices, numbered in terms of their proximity to or distance from the resurrection at dawn. This was the time when jobs for the day were assigned; the abbot gave a talk to provide a spiritual context for the day's work, and saints were named as models for good intention. As preparation for receiving a divine blessing, the monks acknowledged their weakness without God. "I am the blessed beggar and the Lord is passing by this day." The monks leave for work, with a blessing: "May the almighty Lord order your days and doings in his Peace."

TERCE

Terce means "three." It indicates not only the third hour after the resurrection; it is also a celebration of the coming of the Holy Spirit at Pentecost, which happened at this hour. Just as the secular world takes a coffee break, so the monks take a "spirit break." It is an "oasis" for a renewed consecration to the day's work and our proper motivation for it. We also remember that it was during this time that the cross was being constructed for Jesus. This office, as well as the next two, are called the "little hours," since they are short in nature. In the Middle Ages when the offices and psalms were memorized, such pauses could be fulfilled in the hot fields, with a special plea for strength to finish the day.

SEXT

Sext is the sixth hour after the resurrection. Coming at noon, it is a preparation for the central meal of the day. The noonday heat is at its height. Spiritual strengthening comes by remembering Jesus suffering at this time on the cross. We can sense a companionship of suffering. As one tires, one is more prone to distractions, and so the prayer: "Lead us not into temptation."

NONE

The office of None, or ninth, is the hour when Jesus died. One's own fatigue parallels the exhaustion of the cross, and so we participate in the office together. The sun begins to fade, but one must persevere in the task. By encouraging each other, one acts out the meaning of the Church as the Body of Christ, with each part necessary for the whole. The theme could well be Mendelssohn's chorus from *Elijah*: "[The one] that shall endure to the end shall be saved." Anticipating the end of labor brings thoughts of the end of time itself, both for oneself and for all of time.

VESPERS

Vespers is the second of the two major offices of the day. It begins when the first star can be seen, called the vesper star. In the Middle Ages, the Church was at the geographical center of the village, with the homes circling the church, and the fields circling the homes. People could not afford to have fires or even a candle burning all day, but there was always one in the church, symbolizing the "Real Presence" in the tabernacle, which held the consecrated elements of the Eucharist. Vespers is "lighting the lamps," for at the end of the office each family would light a candle from the Christ candle and return to their homes, where the evening meal could well function as a "love feast." The vesper theme is dual—that of thanksgiving in looking back over the day, and a recalling of Eucharist, for in this office the work of one's hands is offered up to God. Sometimes the Eucharist is celebrated at this hour, especially on Thursdays, to reflect Maundy Thursday of Holy Week. Psalms 113-118 are often used here, for they are the hallel psalms that were most likely sung at the Last Supper. The Lord's Supper and the Heavenly Banquet begin to merge. The Magnificat (Luke 1:46-55) is the climax, as a reminder that our work is to be a part of God's labor, in which "he has filled the hungry with good things, and sent the rich

away empty." "Just as you did it to one of the least of these
. . . " (Matt. 25:40).

The feel of this period reminds me of turning into the
driveway, or laborers returning from the fields, and having
a glass of wine together at a fireside with loved ones. We
can universalize vesper time as the desire of each of us to
find the tranquillity of a sacred space, to bring clarity
about one's day. This is the time to let go of the day, finding
peace in the quiet beauty of the evening.

COMPLINE

Compline is Latin for "complete." St. Paul says, "Do
not let the sun go down on your anger, and do not make
room for the devil" (Eph. 4:26-27). This is our
Gethsemane hour, calling for an examination of conscience
and contrition for our faults and neglects. In the growing
darkness, one's hold on one's life is fragile. Since the
monks try to live as Jesus taught, living only one day at a
time, this office is the time for handing back one's life. If
there is someone with whom one needs to make amends,
this is to be done by making peace with each person. An
exercise to get in touch with the inner meaning of
Compline is to review in your mind what you would need
to do or say or write if this truly was the end of your life.
Who would you call and say, "I'm sorry for the misunder-
standing we had. Will you forgive me?" Or "I never told
you how much I appreciate you." By singing this office,
the goal becomes clearer—which is to harmonize, liberate,
and pacify—and in so doing, to make peace with God.

This office is preparation for a guilt-free sleep. The
theme is light and sun, contrasting with night and darkness.
Night is a cloak for the powers of darkness. In the Middle

Ages it was held that after dark, hell is depopulated. Thus the appropriate image is that of frightened chicks, huddling beneath our Mother's wings. "Shelter me in the shadow of your wings." Our prayer of closure is a prayer for all things on earth. Our words are much like Christ's prayers at Gethsemane: "You are in our midst . . . . Do not forsake us." The movement toward completion is summarized in the words of Simeon, who in seeing the Christ child knew that his deepest longings had been fulfilled. And now he and we can pass into God. "Protect us, Lord, as we stay awake; watch over us as we sleep, that awake, we may keep watch with Christ, and asleep rest in his peace." The angels are invited in, that the night might be filled with radiance. The monk's final words are the final words of Jesus: "Into your hands, Lord, I commend my spirit." Then a parting adieu is sung to our heavenly Mother. And the Great Silence begins. Sleep is a symbol of death, and so we hear the abbot's words of blessing: "May the Almighty Lord grant us a restful night and a peaceful death." With an "Amen" as final response, we file to where the abbot stands, near the altar, and are sprinkled with water.

To die is hard, and so to enter the "Great Silence" of death is peaceful only when the sprinkling reminds us of our baptism, when we went beneath the water three times, for the three days in the tomb, and then were brought forth as the resurrection of a new creature. So it is on this special night, for every day is special, one of a kind. Sleeping is a dying, and with the promise of baptism we go to our "cell," now functioning as a death cell, and surrender our life to God. Mary Magdalene's words to Jesus in *Jesus Christ Superstar* often enter my mind: "Let the world turn without you tonight." Monks sleep very well. And if the bell for Vigils rings for me at 3:15 AM, I rise with the words "Christ has risen. He has risen indeed." And with the amazing gift of a brand new day, never before seen or lived, we go to the chapel where at Vigils we once again sing our thankfulness and praise in anticipation.

In living this daily rhythm, I find it helpful to give an image to each of the three-hour segments, as follows:

Vigils: Spirit on the Waters
Lauds: Creation / Resurrection
Prime: Gardeners/Called
Terce: Incarnation / Pentecost
Sext: Exodus / Promised Land
None: Fall / Crucifixion
Vespers: Eucharist / Ascension
Compline: God as All in All

So it is that Jesus taught us to live, only one day at a time, for in so doing one can calm the tyranny of the past, and refuse to permit the future to put us in a state of perpetual postponement. Like Israel in the desert, we are on a daily dole of manna, a gift that will keep for no longer than a day.

Alcoholics Anonymous has captured this fashioning of time in a negative sense, insisting for those enduring the nightmare of quitting alcohol to "live one day at a time." A woman who remembered being struck down by polio expressed how her mother in the hospital taught her how to take still further this approach to time. "If the day is too long for you, try one hour. If this is too much, try one minute. And if you can live it for that long, you can do it for one more—until life is a string of 'just one mores.'"

5. Hourly Time

In the Middle Ages, a practice arose called the *Angelus*. It is a Marian devotion reminiscent of when the angel (i.e., "messenger") Gabriel came to Mary announcing her conception. The bells for the Angelus rang at the beginning, middle, and end of each day, calling people in the fields to pray. This practice has been retained in many monasteries. Yet since those in the secular world have no bells, the equivalent might be the commonplace battery-operated wristwatch. It can be set so that there is a "beep" every hour, on the hour. What could be easier than to pause at the sound and say a short prayer? The theme of the prayer could follow those suggested above. Or one can memorize a prayer, as the Angelus ascribes.

Most people who desire to become more spiritual do rather well at first, in working out their own approach to sacralizing time and space. But the trick then becomes one of remembering to *do* what one has *promised*. Thus reminders are very helpful—indeed, necessary. A note or prayer taped to the bathroom mirror would help so one can easily see it in the morning. Other reminders might be a note at one's place at the table, the refrigerator door, the car dashboard, on one's tools, one's desk, on the bed stand, or at the front door (or even here a dish of water). Then there is no excuse for not doing as one has promised. One can do what Evelyn Underhill calls "darts of prayer"—several words intended for God, perhaps no more than "thank you."

6. Momentary Time

This view of time may be a bit difficult to grasp, but it is really a variation on the adage of stopping to smell the roses. Creation does not mean that God created the universe in the beginning, and then was through with creating. Quite the opposite. God continually creates and recreates, for in each moment one exists because one is upheld by the Mystery that is God. If God would "forget" anything, for even a split second, it simply would no longer be. To be out of the divine presence would mean our complete annihilation. We used the analogy of a light being utterly dependent upon the flow of electricity. So it is with everything that exists. To perceive this is to know that the mere fact that anything exists is sufficient for us to know that God is. Sensing this, perhaps the most characteristic trait that a Christian might develop is thankfulness, realizing that in every moment one lives by gift alone—the sheer grace of life itself.

At this point, we are close to what we will explore in a later work as the sacralizing of space, because attentiveness in each moment to being alive is to awaken, too, to the "giftness" of everything that surrounds one. An exercise that can help at this point is what I call a "monastic walk." This is best done in pairs, with two rules: (1) Speak only when it improves the silence, and (2) Any talking must remain in the present tense. This is very difficult to do, but it is what Jesus taught his disciples—"Do not be anxious about tomorrow, for tomorrow will be anxious for itself" (Matt. 6:34 RSV). We are to live fully and totally in the present, responding thankfully for each breath.

One thing that happens almost immediately on the

monastic walk is typical of the habit we are trying to break. One sees a beautiful flower, and it is so natural to say, "My grandmother used to have one of those in her garden" (past). "I wish I could grow things like that" (future). One must minimize both remembrance and anticipation. If one would set as one's goal the full living of every moment, one's living would be transformed into expansiveness. In a most literal way, it is in God that we live, move, and have our being. To perceive this is to know that the mere fact that anything exists is sufficient for us to know that God is.

7. Time and Timelessness

Much of life is lived in the valley, but for each of us there are special moments. T.S. Eliot speaks about time being "made through that moment,"[10] or "the point of intersection of the timeless."[11] Kelty says that at least once in a lifetime, one's entire life is dependent on a moment. It is often only later that one understands that all other moments were preparation for this moment, from which one's meaning flows. On such moments, one risks one's life. Almost all saints share that timeless moment into and from which their meaningful time flowed. The popularity of the camera rests in the desire to halt time by containing it in a special moment. So it is that Christianity rests on a powerful sense of memory.

The life of Moses serves as an example. His powerful moment occurred in Egypt when he saw a Hebrew slave being beaten. In a moment, his instant response was anger sufficient to kill the Egyptian and bury him in the sand.

193

How long would that take? Perhaps half an hour? Probably less. But he was captured by that moment, and while he tried to run from that moment, he couldn't, for he was branded. Thus he spent the rest of his life seeking liberation for his people. And what was the end, which flowed back to give meaning to the whole? It was when God led Moses to a mountain. It was there that he caught a glimpse of the Promised Land, the goal to which these many years had been dedicated. But he himself would never enter that land. With tear-streaked eyes, how long could he endure the pain of looking? Perhaps half an hour? Here we have the life of one of the great ones, whose life flowed from two events of "timeless time" that totaled less than one hour in length but that had infinite depth.

The "present" is a timeless moment, an invisible line between past and future. This present has the power to redeem the past and the wisdom to discern the novelty impinging from the future. This capacity helps us understand why many of the saints regarded "contemplation" as the highest form of spirituality. An aid in becoming contemplative is repeating continuously a word or phrase (mantra) as a way to empty the mind of both past and future. It is a process of slowing, saying the mantra only as fast as one needs in order to keep the mind occupied. And as the slowing continues, it moves toward a timeless moment, and one's soul is centered at rest. This moment is invaded by the thundering of silence, as one is interpenetrated in the "Nothingness" of a contentless "now." While time and thought are ingredients of the "flow" of time, here in the "now" is a feeling that is warm, intense, and full.

Such centering not only can give birth to a calm center ("soul"), but it can establish a lifestyle in which a person can be intensely focused in the here and now, whatever one is doing. One can sense such a centered person, identifiable by an openness to otherness. Contemplative persons invite what is "now before them" to enter them so they are absorbed by it—for example, a flower, tree, or another person. What happens is a profound mutuality, an immersion. Here it is that life becomes an openness to the world's speaking out, whether in crying out, calling out, singing out, or hoping forth.

This timeless present is living in the tension between memory and vision. And the way this is done renders each person unique, just as Scripture testifies that each "star differs from star in glory" (1 Cor. 15:41). Christian hermits, in attempting to be God-like, attempt to stay only in the present moment, as does God. In being neither past nor future, one lives, at least in foretaste, the immensity of the eternal. My spiritual director lives in this way—for hours on end he remains in the presence of God. His way of expressing time is, "I'm just passing through." His description of me is that I become immersed in everything along the path. Hopefully there is a place for both of us in approaching time.

8. Ordinary Time

Ordinary time totals thirty-three or thirty-four weeks of the church year. It begins the Monday after Epiphany and continues through the Tuesday before Ash Wednesday. It resumes when the Easter Season ends, on the day after Pentecost, until the beginning of Advent, on the fourth Sunday before Christmas. In a very real sense the special

195

times we have explored function much like dress rehearsals for living in "real" time, when in a kind of "soloing" one attempts to live ordinary time in an extraordinary way. Abraham Heschel wisely affirmed that to be human consists in outbursts of singularity. It is in ordinary time that such singularity is welcomed.

Another way of discerning the meaning of "ordinary time" is to recall the important function that Sunday has for the Christian. Every seven days, the Sabbath is celebrated as a "little Easter." The two great yearly liturgical seasons that we have explored are efforts to expand the celebrations of particular aspects of the weekly Eucharistic celebrations. Thus ordinary time is not very ordinary at all, since the weekly celebrations of the Resurrection are ongoing reminders of how to live eucharistically. Sunday, as the intertwining of play and worship, has rightfully been called a sacrament of redeemed time. With such a model, ordinary time is when we do the dishes, buy groceries, chauffeur the children, show up at the office or classroom—when we do all these "ordinary" things *for God*. And by so doing, we experience a joy that renders all things sacramental. Through this understanding of the pyramid of time that we have been sharing, from cosmic time downward through the year to each day, and finally to the moment—all of these form the intricate web through which our dependence on God becomes gloriously alive.

This brings us to the focus of the human dilemma. It is crucial to be able to pause attentively, captured by the intensity of the moment, as if there will never be one like it. There will not be. Never. This means living at the edge of tremendous loss. We miss this sacred urgency when we live in an illusion that we have unlimited time. This was why the medieval monks practiced *memento mori*. With a skull on the desk before them, they meditated upon the imminence of their death. For the rest, Ash Wednesday entailed being anointed with the dust of cremation, as it were. Through the urgency born of limit, one is enabled to celebrate the fragments of the mundane as tokens of mystery and delight. The existentialist novelists, such as Albert Camus, saw sleepwalking as a primary sin. This is the condition from which our painful behavior follows.

Thornton Wilder's *Our Town* portrays this condition. Grover's Corners is *my* town, and thus *our* town— Wherever, USA. Emily dies but is permitted to leave the grave for one last visit. She chooses to re-enter on her twelfth birthday. "Oh, Mama, just look at me one minute as though you really saw me." These words bring tears to my own eyes. The town is South Fork, and it is to my mother too that Emily speaks: "Mama, just for a moment. We're happy. Let's look at one another."[12] Or the plea is directed to my father and me. Several weeks before his death by cancer, my daughter Kathy visited him. She summarized her visit in five words: "Paul, he never knew you." This human condition was too much for Emily too: "I can't go on." "All that was going on and we never noticed."

But she cannot refrain from looking back, for now she *has* been bitten by seeing, truly. Good-bye to the sunflowers, food, coffee, dresses, baths, sleeping, waking—especially waking. "Do any human beings ever realize life while they live it? Every, every minute?" Wilder suggests that saints and poets might. Yet how many poets were burned by coming too close, or saints by standing on the edge of "too-much." But to be awakened, if only once, is to be called to embrace the fragments and to kiss the toad into prince-hood. Cornel West's phrase is an evocative one: to be called to "subversive joy." To live ordinary time with the eyes to see is to live in a world that "is indeed a wild, holy place."[13] It is in these melodies of praise, in the ebb and flow of our days and hours, that we may sing of God as the beloved friend of all our seasons.

9. The God of Time

This multidimensional nature of time is finally rooted in the nature of God. Time is real not only for us but for God as well, for in the Christ event God himself entered time and blessed it. In an important sense, because of Pentecost, we can speak of the Holy Spirit as existence itself, the common denominator of all that is. Eastern thought portrays the consummation of our relationship with God as our becoming lost in cosmic consciousness. Western thought, by contrast, portrays our relationship with God as that of cosmic lover, as the soul's bridegroom. Thus relationship is central to life and is the goal of living itself: to love God for God's own sake. To approach this relation with the necessary humility, all imagery must bow before the apophatic approach to God, which is the acknowledgment that God as the Absolute is beyond all images that can be thought or spoken. Ultimately God is never "this" nor "that." God is No-thing, and No-where. Yet God is, as St. Bernard claimed, inclusive of all length, breadth, height, and depth. And still we continue to "seek the face of God," a phrase sprinkled widely throughout Scripture.

Consequently, the center of Christian revelation is that although God is utterly transcendent, in Jesus Christ we do indeed perceive the "face of God." Thus we can declare that the transcendent God is also lovingly *immanent* in superabundance. God is the ground of endless self-giving, so that even God's enemies are loved. Augustine said this another way, identifying God as the only reality, so that we are real only insofar as we are in God, and God is in us. We can even speak of the corporeality of God—that God's body includes everything, while the Church as the Body of Christ reveals everything. The universe is the temple of God, and the Church is its altar.

God is with us, for us, in us—as us. So related is God to Creation that Scripture portrays God as thirsting for us, suffering over our estrangement. As Jesus Christ, God becomes a pilgrim and exile in creation; thus we can speak of the loneliness of God, a God who longs for our friendship. Ironically, God reveals God's self in hiddenness as One unknown. And yet, while working in the world incognito, Christ becomes the "spectacles" by which we can recognize God everywhere. And what we recognize is that Christ is the Messiah for whom all humankind yearns, and the Christ is no other than God. Most of the time, the original disciples and we do not recognize God as present—until afterwards. For the Jews, God's presence in their history occurred to them as they sat around campfires in Babylon, dreaming of Zion. So it was that only after his death, as the disciples broke bread and drank wine together in the upper room, did they know Christ as profoundly present.

In both cases, it was like reading history backwards. The most profound of gifts are the images we are given by which to continue to read the history of God backwards.

Thus in our imagination we have a hunch that the inwardness of the cosmos is the "heaven" where God dwells, and the outwardness of all creation is in God, for God is the One in whom we live and move and have our being. God is the abiding Source as well as the Sum of reality. "If I ascend to heaven, you are there" (Ps. 139:8). Put another way, the Son is the heart of the Father, who in Creation is bringing birth to that which is like him. As to the future, God is the totality of our world that in fullness is yet to come. Underhill illustrates this well in speaking of God as an artist fashioning the creation, so that each human spirit is an unfinished work of art

Expressed another way, Incarnation is the affirmation that all things, living and nonliving, everything alive or dead, is created and sustained and consummated *by* God and *in* God. But there is another side to the Christian's understanding of God. Merton affirmed that the wounds of the sepulchre are taken into God. During his death, Resurrection, and Ascension, Christ remains both God and human as well. This is a powerful part of the good news. God takes the sufferings and joys of people into God's own self, and as divine experiences, they are never lost, but become part of God's very life and love. For so many who are fearful lest their living is in vain, resurrection and ascension are the promise that nothing shall be futile or lost.

Elijah experienced God in two ways, as do we: (1) as womb of the still, small voice and (2) as the Lord of history. The first way is characteristic of the contemplative, in which we are alone in the aloneness of the Alone. Holy Saturday expresses this mystery of the "death" or "absence" of the God who is hidden. In the second way,

200

God is revealed not only in time, but God is also partisan, taking our side, working in terms of "weighted invitations." God is the incarnate surging in everything, the creative yearning, as God's fingers touch gently the edges of God's becoming. To declare Christ to be God is to affirm that the central events of his life disclose the inmost nature of God. In whatever way God enters our lives, for those who are honest about themselves, it is always a miracle of overwhelming compassion. Some are called to ponder God, others to vanish into God, some to feel God, and others to translate God's yearnings into action. In whichever way, God is the Majestic Mystery, the Crucified One who nonetheless plays in his world by dancing.

10. End Time and Death

Everyone and everything that exists has a specter blocking the doorway—the one called Death. All time in this life shall end, either as a pathetic finality or as threshold to what shall be. Merton suggests that our incessant talk is an attempt to hold off death, and understandably so, for honesty would suggest that a death sentence is probably the proper judgment call on each of us. And yet the scriptural portrait surrounding Christ's death suggests that just as the Temple veil was torn by his dying, so the veil will be torn open for us at the moment of our death.

But death is not simply reserved for the end. Ever since some point in our teens, our bodies have been relentlessly deteriorating. Tillich said that death is not only the scissors that cuts life's thread, but it is the thread woven into the very fabric of life. Freud speaks of a death wish, and

Merton refers to the death dance in our blood. In Vietnam, death became a terror staring out at every soldier from every doorway. All one could hope for was just to get out alive. So it is understandable that more medals were given in Vietnam than there were soldiers. In strong contrast to such carnage, Christians have tucked away somewhere in the deepest recesses of our souls that only "martyrdom" can redeem the personal pathos of Time. The feast day of each saint is thus observed on the date of their death, for that is their beginning.

But all of us, in the end, have no way out. Death blocks the only door. So the question is not "whether" but "how." And the "how" has a major and haunting question before it: Is death God's idea? Or is death God's "foe?" Socrates' "suicide" was a calm and tranquil one. He drank the hemlock. And as his friends cried over his approaching demise, Socrates declared that it is he who should be crying for them. His soul was going home, to a place from which he had been exiled at birth, while they still had more living to do.

Christians, however, having Jesus as our supreme model, have a remarkably different perspective. At Gethsemane, Jesus went alone to God in prayer, three times, pleading for God to remove the cup of death from him. And as he did so, his sweat was like drops of blood. The torture he endured robbed him of any heroism, for he could not even carry his own cross. And as death's grim sneer came closer, he screamed out, "My God, my God, why have you forsaken me?" (Mark 15:34). Clearly, then, *death is not God's idea.* It is God's foe, against which he pitted his own Son. And with Christ's resurrection came the victory—that in all cases, the God of life will have the last word. This is no affirmation of the immortality of the soul. It is the full promise of Resurrection of the "body"— not of flesh or of some part of us, but in the fullness of who we are and in a wholeness we shall attain through Christ. In the face of Alzheimer's, the promise is almost too good to be true. But if there now is with God the Father the enfleshed One who walked the Palestine roads, then we can shout the Easter claim: "Death, where is your sting?"

Yet while envisaging one's own death is hard to do, choosing martyrdom is even harder to imagine. In fact, to do so for the right reasons becomes possible only when we realize that in one's baptism one's death has already been "died" with Christ, and we have already risen with him. In being free to die, one's whole life comes into focus. We are the most precious gifts that God can be given. The issue no longer is "if" or "when," but "how" and "why." Braaten concludes that the only free person is one not hung up with his own dying. There is some sadness shared by the monks when one of their brothers dies, for they will miss him. But I am amazed that the fundamental emotion is joy, for the veil has opened. Death is the heavenly birthday, and from henceforth they will be remembered not on their birthdays when they entered life, but on the birthday of their dying into eternal life.

The burial hole in the cemetery is a chalice, into which our brother is gently placed after a final embrace. The monk's cowl is pulled up over his face. There is no coffin. There is nothing there, except the body of our brother. His feet are pointed toward the rising sun, whenceforth comes Christ's resurrection and return. Slowly we take turns covering our brother with earth, beginning at his feet and moving toward his head, as if "tucking" him in for a deep sleep. If God can transform little disks that look like fish food into his very body, so too can this Eucharistic God work his "transubstantiation" with our brother. Christians must do their living in the full face of death's inevitability. All we have is God's promise in Jesus Christ. *But it is enough.* Returning from the cemetery, our chanting is our steadfast belief in the Christian vision—that resurrection is the meaning of all Time.

CHAPTER SEVEN

The Triduum

"My one companion is darkness." (Ps. 88:19 GRAIL)
"You have turned my mourning into dancing." (Ps. 30:11)
"A day in your courts is better than a thousand elsewhere." (Ps. 84:10)

The meaning of all Creation and all of time depends on the primal image through which one views faith. A number of triads have been used in the Church's tradition, such as these triadic themes:

Birth / Fall / Rebirth
Crucifixion / Resurrection / Ascension
Transcendence / Immanence / Incarnation
Garden / Exile / Kingdom
Home / Far Country / Homecoming

Although the age of our cosmos is measured in billions of years, the Church has known for centuries that the Christian faith is inextricably tied to *three days* (the Triduum) within that vast expanse—Maundy Thursday, Good Friday, and Easter. Even the rich imagery of the Church's themes that have arisen through the centuries are finally tested for their authentic meaning in the Triduum, which the Church celebrates as the center point of all time and space. Inward renewal for each of us, it turns out, is integrally tied to walking annually these three sacred days as a pilgrimage. They are the foundation, out of which the Eucharist arises as the Image of images. The Triduum is the special time when the events of God's activity are invited to walk around in us.

1. Maundy Thursday: The Radiance of Opposites

During the Dark Ages, monasteries preserved this heart of the gospel. So it may be today. I remember indelibly my first monastic Triduum. The Trappist monastery was nestled in the Ozark Hills adorned with dogwood. The chapel on that Maundy Thursday was a portrait in contrasts. The tabernacle, where the reserved host is traditionally treasured, gaped open—empty, as if robbed, too late to lock the barn door. Nevertheless, daffodils, dogwood, and redbud flooded the area around the altar. But the hope was strained, for in the center of the flowers was a crown of thorns. Yet, ironically, the thorns rested on a silk pillow. But its color was purple. This bombardment of the imagination, it turned out, was the necessary initiation for the Triduum as a *symbol feast*.

The mood of the service was likewise paradoxical. While the opening confession and absolution were somber continuations of Lenten preparation, the tower bell suddenly pealed as the monks chanted the Gloria. Yet there was little joy. The sound was that of a farewell song for a departing friend. Then all became subdued, for neither bell nor Gloria would sound again, ever, unless—if one dared believe it—the Resurrection would somehow occur again. This is why "Alleluia" is a word forbidden throughout the six weeks of Lent, preserved as the only fitting response if the Gloria should ever again proclaim as fact the center point of history: "He is risen!"

In the interim, with bell ropes tightly tied, the only sound to call us to prayer would be the rattle of Ezekiel's dry bones (Ezek. 37:1-14). Made ready by our Lenten immersion in Israel's longing, we heard the Passover promise. But the real homily was a sign-event reenacting the New Testament reading. Becoming the Christ who "emptied himself, taking the form of a servant" (Phil. 2:7), the abbot removed all his vestiges of authority. Vested only with an apron, he washed the feet of each monk, drying them with a kiss. Humbling was the profound contrast between such gentleness and the kiss of betrayal that we would soon give with Judas.

The irony continued, for the dynamic of the liturgy refused to let us dwell in such sadness. The mood turned almost jubilant in the recognition that the Christ, soon to be betrayed, had made provision for us so that we would never suffer without him the abandonment he soon would face because of us. On this night, Christ instituted the Eucharist, on a table such as any kitchen table, so that the God incarnate in history would become incarnate in us, again and again, in the bread and wine of his Real Presence. The miracle of this night was that the "Last Supper" two thousand years ago was to become the "Lord's Supper" now.

I had come to this monastic Triduum with serious doubts. My scientific mind knew that dead persons do not rise. Furthermore, I had just finished a book by a Harvard theologian explaining the Easter experience as "hallucination." Little of my childhood faith remained. But on that Maundy Thursday—in graphic contrast to the scientific, psychological, and individualistic language inculturated into my head—I encountered this intensely corporate, dramatic, symbolic, and liturgical language-event. Instead of "demythologizing," explaining, or justifying anything, I was being invited to participate in the originating event whereby the resurrection of Christ is "known in the breaking of bread." I began to discover what my later searching of the Scriptures was to confirm—that almost every resurrection appearance occurred as the faithful were eating and drinking together. This Triduum was my invitation into the resurrection "miracle," through which a simple chapel in the Ozark Hills was to become the empty tomb by way of the "upper room." I sensed in a new way how much hung on that simple piece of bread lifted into my gaze as both affirmation and question: "The body of Christ!?" Resurrection is the gift of being able to answer, "Amen!"

After communing, the abbot completed the Lord's Supper by delivering Jesus' final sermon to his disciples (John 17). At its climax, affirmation again became question: Is it true that the Father and Jesus are one, so that the life and death of Jesus is the life and death of God? "When they had sung a hymn, they went out to the Mount of Olives" (Matt. 26:30). As we sang, perhaps the same psalm as they, the abbot embraced tightly the lidded chalice ("ciborium") containing Eucharistic bread sufficient only for our final meal—on death row, as it were, awaiting with Christ our Good Friday execution. Israel's "Holy of Holies" was veiled, and so regularly is the monastic tabernacle. But this time the veil was placed around the abbot-priest. He, and all of us who had communed, became the tabernacle. As Moses led the Passover people out of Egypt, so now the priest "as Christ" led us through the "Jerusalem gate" into the secret place known to Jesus and his disciples. Monks, guests, passersby—we moved through the dark halls into the forbidden cloistered area of the monastery, like a requiem column, toward the "garden" chapel. There the ciborium was placed in our own Gethsemane. This is where Jesus went a little ways off, returning with a question: "Could you not stay awake with me one hour?" (Matt. 26:36-46). Some of us did, until one by one, we slipped quietly away to sleep.

Several hours later, we reassembled for Compline. Our desertion became graphic. The main chapel was now totally stripped, as if a thief had come by night while we failed to keep watch. The only illumination was a harsh light under a relentless clock. The only object was the crown of thorns, apparently tossed under the communion table as if not worth stealing. The real benediction occurred, however, as I walked out into the Ozark night. The first whippoorwill of spring sang, as I ached. It appeared that meaning was to come, if at all, in the radiance of opposites.

2. Good Friday: The Fragile Edge of Faith

I experienced that Good Friday as the most honest day of the Christian year. It is when the "desert temptations" become unavoidable. Even Jesus tasted them—the enticements of power, possession, and prestige. *When faced with death, we all have our price.* The monks observe this day in melancholy silence, as if the world stood on tiptoe, holding its breath for fear of being dropped. This Friday, ironically called "good," is one of bread and water and bare feet, a day of consuming our final morsels of communion bread, a day when we are left with not even crumbs under the table. The liturgy that morning centered in the fourteen psalms of sadness and regret, necklaced by a continuation of the week's readings from Lamentations. Nothing was chanted, for there was no longer anything about which to sing. There were only the sad words, themselves read as if each syllable were shrouded.

At 3:00 PM, with bare feet against cold floors, the experience was of death's finality. The priest's vestment was blood red with a black cross woven into the fabric. The crucifixion story from John's Gospel was chanted as a requiem, three monks becoming the characters. With the words "He gave up his spirit" (John 19:30), we prostrated ourselves. Spread-eagle against the hard floor, as each of us became the crucifix, I sensed the terror of being cosmically alone, inadequate to my final core. The tombstone for everything read: "My God, My God, why have you forsaken me?" (Matt. 27:46).

Rising from the floor, we stood facing the "dead God," dangling above us on a cross, like a plucked chicken hanging from a butcher's hook. With utter absurdity, we prayed to this Dead One. For at least ten minutes we interceded for the whole of creation. No one was excluded: people of other faiths, people of no faith, the church, the state, the sick, the dying, even the politicians—all were lifted up onto that cross in behavior defying all logic. Everything was made to depend on who this figure is: a pitiful Nazarene peasant, prefiguring our common fate, or the abandoned God who refuses to abandon us. Whoever you are, "Into your hands I commend my spirit!" (Luke 23:46).

"Are ye able," goes the old hymn, "to be crucified with me?" The crucifix was readied, as if for a test run. One by one we moved through the silence to kiss the feet of the Crucified. The head of the nail was cold against my lips. I let my teeth check its hardness. This was for real. Dying into nothingness, or gambling on the resurrection of the dying God. In that choice *the* paradox was given a name and a face.

"Can God spread a table in the wilderness?" a skeptical Israel taunted (Ps. 78:19). In reply, the priest went to the Gethsemane chapel and brought back to our naked table the only hope left. "Even though I walk through the valley of the shadow of death, . . . Thou preparest a table before me in the presence of Death my enemy" (Ps. 23:4-5, my alteration). Its frail appearance was that of a stale, leftover cardboard wafer. Yet the priest held it before me, eye to eye: "The body of Christ!?" The presence of absence, or the Absence as Presence. "Amen." "I believe; help my unbelief!" (Mark 9:24). The communion bread was gone. I walked outside into a twilight that orchestrated this fragile, exhilarating edge of faith in the face of nothingness. After a lifetime of self-responsibility, self-reliance, self-everything, I sensed what it might mean to relinquish control, forfeiting the need for self-justification.

The monks' final office each night is Compline. In the darkness, one hands back the life that God gives, one day at a time. Courage to enter the nightly "death chamber" of one's "cell" comes when the abbot sprinkles each monk, as we bow before the crucifix. Recalling that in our baptism we were buried with Christ and *raised with Christ,* we enter the "Great Silence," knowing that our death no longer awaits, but is behind us. After this, my first Good

Friday Compline, I fell asleep with the words: "If we live, we live to the Lord, and if we die, we die to the Lord; so then, whether we live or whether we die, we are the Lord's" (Rom. 14:8).

3. Holy Saturday: Living Between the Times

Holy Saturday, as an extension of Good Friday, began with the death rattle of shaken bones. With the tabernacle uninhabited, the bread of sustenance devoured, the candles extinguished, the music gone, and the hunger growing, the liturgy pushed toward the final desert step into Nothingness. This Saturday seemed to distill our society, a living between the times: "Now is too late for action, too soon for contrition."[1] The monks had two options. When the bottom fell out, the disciples reverted to work—they went fishing (John 21:3). The second choice was to take a hermit day—wrapping oneself in a baptismal shroud, as it were, contemplating one's own death. Either way, those of us who were homesick at home yearned to be alone without loneliness.

4. Easter Day: Through Death into Life

Easter Vigil began at 3:15 AM. The monks emerged from the monastery like white shadows, into the tangible silence of the darkness. We huddled around an open fire, much as Peter did when he insisted with chattering teeth, "I never knew him!" Carving a cross on a huge Paschal Candle, the abbot inscribed an Alpha at its head, an

Omega at its foot. Then he carved into the cross the numbers of our year in salvation history. At this point the Christian perspective on time reaches perhaps its climax, for as he inscribes the priest proclaims these words:

Christ yesterday and today
The beginning and the end
Alpha
And Omega
All time belongs to him
And all the ages
To him be glory and power
Through every age forever.
Amen.

Then using five grains of incense as nails, the abbot pressed Christ's wounds, which are our doing, into the wax of time. And from these "glorious wounds" "may the light of Christ dispel the darkness."

It is with heavy irony that this candle, hope of our new beginnings, was ignited from the campfire of betrayal. Like Israel before us, it became our pillar of fire by night. "Christ our light," chanted the priest. "Thanks be to God," came our hesitant echo. He paused at the chapel door, as if his courage flagged. He offered the Paschal flame to our unlit candles. Then, with the night ablaze, we dared enter the deserted chapel of the crucifixion.

In a blaze of candlelight, the chanted first words of the liturgy said it all: "On this most holy night . . . our Lord Jesus Christ passed from death to life . . . [so] that we shall share his victory over death and live with him forever in God." With the individual candles blended into one light, so did nine Scripture readings become a mosaic of common pilgrimage—from the drama of creation, through the Red Sea, into the desert, through the Promised Land, toward God's gift of the Messiah. This was the pilgrimage by which we the betrayers were to become the Rock against which the "powers of death shall not prevail" (Matt. 16:18 RSV).

The silent tower bells suddenly erupted in anticipation. We responded with "Gloria in Excelsis," as the Christmas promise became the resurrection fulfillment. A second excitement greeted the New Testament proclamation, as "Alleluias" pent-up for six weeks burst forth. Sung in groupings of three, twelve in all, even the Alleluias glowed with symbolism.

Suddenly the movement of the liturgy reversed as anticipation became appropriation. Christ's Passover in history became our personal pilgrimage into resurrection through the waters of our baptism. Together we relived the sacred stories of water—the gift of creation, the flood of judgment, the Red Sea of liberation, the Jordan of calling, and the water of redemption flowing from Christ's pierced side. The connection of baptism and resurrection became graphic as the huge Paschal Candle was plunged three times into the baptismal water and raised on the third. As crescendo, the angels were evoked and twenty-seven saints beckoned by name, and finally all of them were invited: "All holy men and women," past and present. "Surrounded by so great a cloud of witnesses" (Heb.12:1), we were sprinkled in a baptismal re-passing through death into life.

Assured that our death had died, the Eucharist became a resurrection breakfast. As the disciples first ate with the resurrected Christ on the lake shore (John 21:12), so now the dead God greeted us as Real Presence. "Christ the Lord Is Risen Today" was the hymn as we exited—not into the morning darkness, but right on through the cloister, straight into the kitchen. There the Lenten fast was broken, with the gooiest and most decadent cinnamon rolls that loving hands could make.

The mid-morning Eucharist of the Resurrection related to the Easter Vigil much as Confirmation relates to Baptism. To the resurrection announcement that our lives "never again shall see darkness," the renewal of baptismal vows became a recommissioning of the resurrection people on behalf of the whole cosmos to which resurrection has been promised. We prayed that the God who had "given us a new birth by water and the Holy Spirit" might now "keep us faithful."

Jesus' emptying of his will in God's became the paradigm of human existence itself. And in the Triduum, this distillation becomes the absolute revelation of the nature of time itself.

5. God's Final Word

My first monastic Triduum occurred well over a decade ago. This Easter, it was I who preached the homily at the Resurrection Eucharist. What can one add to a liturgy that celebrates the resurrection promise into fact? I tried. The Scripture for the day was simple enough: the story of two disciples running to a vacant tomb, then returning to their homes (John 20:1-10). For them, I suggested, the resurrection had not yet occurred—for when it does, one can never go home again. Even Judas could not escape the Easter event. He hanged himself. But tradition tells us that on Holy Saturday Jesus "descended into hell." This time it must have been Jesus who kissed Judas, repeating the same words as in the garden: "Friend, why are you here?" But this time they became a resurrection invitation to Judas: "Follow me." Jesus knows the way out, even out of hell. Together they walked, and all of creation walked with them—through the Red Sea to death's other side. If at Easter the slaughtered lamb becomes the Good Shepherd, then God's final word to everything must be "Yes!" (2 Cor.1:19).

Three hours, three days, three years, three lifetimes, three millennia—makes no difference. When we touch these three days, we touch the innermost meaning of everything. One thing more. St. Paul spoke of God this way: "It is the God who said, 'Let light shine out of darkness' [the Creator], who has shone in our hearts [Holy Spirit] to give the light of the knowledge of the glory of God in the face of Jesus Christ" (2 Cor. 4:6). Our three days give us not only the way to live the various dimensions of time. They correlate as well with the very nature of God as triune—the Lord of Time.

CHAPTER EIGHT

Conclusion

Over the years, I have explored most approaches to spirituality and participated in many. As a Christian I have come to appreciate those which have profound respect for the emergence of mind and self-consciousness as distinguishing marks of being human. This is to insist that Christian life be insatiably wrapped in time, as rooted in the enfleshment of the Incarnation, the carnality of the Crucifixion, the temporal restoration of the Resurrection, and the concrete increase through Ascension. In Coptic there is a single word for heart and mind; if only there were in English we might better be able to grasp the reality of living time.

Perhaps through Eastern influences, current talk about spirituality stresses the timeless—and with it minimizes the miracle of mind and perceives self-consciousness as intrusive and distractive. Lest I be misunderstood, there is in me a deep yearning finally to become lost in God, with contemplative foretastes along the way. And yet I insist that the journey is as important as the arrival. One needs to pray not only with one's eyes clenched closed, but also vibrantly open. One philosopher was asked which he would choose: the gift of all wisdom, or the search for it. He—and I too—chose the latter.

As I have mentioned, my spiritual director, a hermit, once smiled at me and concluded: "The difference between the two of us is that, while life for me is a matter of passing through, for you it is a matter of drinking deeply of everything along the way." True. I do not want to miss the aroma of even one wild strawberry along the path. That is, *I want to live deeply in time in all its manifold richness.*

Perhaps it was because I was younger then, but I often remember an experience with an Atlanta elevator. At a conference in a hotel there, some friends suggested that as an "adventure" I ride with them in a glass elevator to the top. Slowly it rose, as I took in the gothic-like panorama beneath: of water features, plants, chandeliers, and colorful people of all kinds. Suddenly we burst through the roof into momentary darkness, then into a glass tube, where stretching out in all directions were the lights of Atlanta's skyline and above it, the trek of endless stars. While still mesmerized, we penetrated through a floor into a sphere at the top. And as the doors opened, a friendly voice, with a warm handshake, bid us come and eat.

That night, at a table slowly rotating above the glittering city below, we told stories of past, present, and future. That was when I knowingly celebrated for the first time that I was a joyful denizen of time. Even the infinite space all around was bathed in time. Just that morning I had read that an astronomer had perceived a quark twelve billion light-years hence. Staggered by it all, that night I toasted the God of time, drinking thankfully for being alive in all of time's multifarious intersections. Most important of all, I received an assurance that a Christian approach to spirituality does not call for a forfeiture of the flesh. The Mystery has a face. Because of all, and in spite of all, I laughed, deeply, over the things of time—above all over the joy simply of being. Or was it a childlike giggle? Whichever, it made no difference. *I was in love with the God "who visits us like the dawn from on high"* (Luke 1:78).[1]

Years later, I know now the appeal of my brother Trappist, Fr. Matthew Kelty. While he too tastes well the timelessness of silence, he knows as well the temporal richness of time lived as a poem. His epiphany came on a spring morning, "as beautiful as God ever made." Birds sang in wild abandon; two horses frolicked in the wet grass; breeze and clouds abounded—everything. "And who was playing most or best?" Each was playing, all in their own ways, in a joyous joining of earth with heaven. So it no longer mattered to Matthew that in chapel the pitch had been high and the choir flat, and he had been mad. All were singing now with the angels—"every person on earth: the good and the bad, the virtuous and the dissolute, the sober and the drunken, the free and the imprisoned, the rich and the poor, people dying and leaving the world, people being born and just coming into it. I sing with them all in Christ." To enter time well requires only that we play unselfishly, as a little child, and thus become "lost in rapture at the great reality that lies hidden just under the surface of everything."[2]

For some persons the quest for the Absolute means closing one's eyes and ears to the carnival, but for me, in memory and in imagination, it means taking it all into me as a gift into God. As Bach labored mightily on his *magnum opus*, "The Art of the Fugue," he felt the presence of death. So he stopped, in the middle of a musical phrase, and from his deathbed he dictated the choral prelude, "Before Thy Throne I Stand." It was his prayer that he could take it with him, as a final gift. Before that throne, I expect to be asked a question something like this: "Have you drunk deeply of time, known its beauty, and shared it all?"

APPENDICES

"I remember the days that are past. . . .
Make me know the way I should walk . . . ."
(Ps. 143:5, 8 GRAIL)

The following appendices offer some
practices the reader can use as means
of sacralizing time.

APPENDIX ONE

Recollection Exercise
for Spiritual Direction

For use with individuals or with groups.

For each of the following questions, write the very first thing that comes to mind:

1. If you could go anywhere in the world and bring back from there a symbol of who you are, what would that OBJECT be?

2. Where is HOME for you? It can be anything from a place, a rocking chair, or an activity.

3. Identify your favorite TOWN or CITY. Why?

4. A. If you were at an overnight workshop and there is a two-hour break, where would a friend who knows you well come looking for you?
   B. Does that ASSOCIATION please you? If not, what place would you prefer for friends to associate you with?

5. A. What COLOR best expresses what it feels like to be inside you?
   B. What color do you most likely project to others?

6. Where is your favorite place to go when you want to dream?

7. What kind of BUILDING best characterizes the influence of your past on you?

8. What ACTIVITY are you doing when you are most yourself?

9. A. What ANIMAL represents best the way folks probably tend to see you?
   B. What animal best represents the way you tend to see yourself?

10. Whom do you most ADMIRE?

11. A. What would you secretly like to DO?
    B. What would you secretly like to BE?

12. What BIBLICAL FIGURE do you most identify with?

13. Chose a number (10 is high and 1 is low) that reflects how you are at this point in your journey.

A Daily Office

A daily "Breviary" I have written to use in celebrating time through the five major daily offices: Vigils (Arising), Lauds (Morning), Sext (Noonday), Vespers (Sundown), Compline (Bedtime).

Vigils [Upon Arising]

O God, come to my assistance.
O Liberator, make haste to help us.

O God, you must be my God, for I long, I yearn, I ache.
   Is it not for you that my soul is thirsting?
My body pines like a dry, weary land without water,
   For the vision of our cosmos grasped by your Sabbath
   glory.
I hunch that to be loved unconditionally by your Love is
better than life itself.

God, may I believe in the graciousness of your Grace,
   And have faith in your faithfulness.
Then shall my life be a song of your praise.

On my bed this night I remembered your promises.
   On you I mused through the quiet hours, and I wondered.
O God, be my help.
   In such hope this day, I promise to you the works of

My hands,
    My imagination,
        My relating,
            My dreaming.

O that my soul might be filled—as with a banquet,
    Just as your cosmos yearns for its homecoming.
May I stand in the shadow of your soaring wings,
    That my soul may cling faithfully to the vision we
    saw together—
From Sinai,
    from Pisgah,
        from Golgotha.
            Lord I believe; help thou my unbelief.

And now, in this silence, give us the illumination to
ponder your promise
    Of a new heaven and a new earth.
Let us hear that great voice saying:
    "Behold the dwelling place of God is with humankind.
    God will dwell with them, and they shall be God's
    people.
    God will wipe away every tear from their eyes,
    And death shall be no more,
    Neither shall there be mourning nor crying nor pain
    anymore—
    For the former things have passed away."

"Behold I make all things new.
    To the thirsty I will give water without a price.
Let those who hear say 'Come.'
    And let those who thirst come.

226

And those who desire, receive the water of life without price."

Praise to you this day, O *Creator* of all possibilities.
Dispel the chaos from our lives, that we may know the purity of heart to will one thing:
> The City of God on earth as it is now prefigured in heaven.

Praise to you this day, O *Redeemer* of Life.
> Pardon and accept us unconditionally,
>> That we may no longer be tempted to pretend that we are what we are not.

Praise to you this day, O *Promiser* of final victory.
> Faithful to your promise, strengthen us
> That we may be so blessed by this silence with you
That we may faithfully oppose the demonic systems and powers
> That surround and invade us.

Help us to lose our taste for possessions,
> And power
>> And prestige.
Free us to march to the sound of a different drummer.
Lord we are not worthy to receive you,
But only say the word and we shall be healed.

May the Divine Assistance remain always with us—
> And with our sisters and brothers in the struggle everywhere—
That Justice and Peace may embrace and kiss.

May we not be disappointed in you, although you
have been with us.

All this we pray—
    In the name of Yahweh,
        The martyrs of Christ's revolution,
            The new heaven and the new earth,
        As it was promised in the beginning,
    Must be now,
And will be forever.
Amen.

Lauds [Morning]

This is the day, O Yahweh, which you have made.
    Let us rejoice and be glad in it.
With our bodies refreshed by sleep, we arise.
    O God, open our lips
    That our mouths may proclaim your praise.

Yahweh, you are clothed in beauty, this earth the work of
your hands.
    Sing unto the Lord, all you lands.
    Serve the Lord with gladness.
    Come before our God with joyful song
    Knowing that the Spirit is God.
She has made us, and we are hers.
We are God's people, the flock God tends.

All you waters,
    Bless Yahweh's name.
Sun and moon,
    Bless Yahweh's name.
Stars of heaven,
    Bless Yahweh's name.
Every shower and dew and snow,
    Bless Yahweh's name.
All the winds, heat and cold,
    Bless Yahweh's name.
Light and darkness,
    Bless Yahweh's name.
Mountains and plains,
    Bless Yahweh's name.
Every animal and fish and insect,
    Bless Yahweh's name.
All of us,
    Bless Yahweh's name.

Faithful Emmanuel, send us forth into your world,
    Knowing that in your companionship
        We will never again be lonely,
            Nor powerless,
                Nor unaccepted,
                    Nor rejected,
                        Nor abandoned,
                            Nor of no consequence,
                              Nor without meaning —

For you are indelibly with us,
    As you make our history your own.

And so to the work of this day we turn,
  As those who are under your promises.
God, may I be no longer mine, but yours.
  Put me to what you will, rank me with whom you will.
Put me to doing, put me to suffering.
  Let me be employed for you, or laid aside for you.
Let me be full; let me be empty.
  Let me have all things, let me have nothing.
I freely and heartily yield all things to your pleasure and
disposal.

Be with our Sisters and Brothers in the struggle for justice
and peace.
  But be as well with our contemplative Sisters and
  Brothers,
  Wrapped in prayer,
  Interceding for the World.
May all of us rise this morning in new strength and
determined faithfulness.
Be with those in affliction and captivity—let their cry
come to you.
  Sweep away their pain and agony, that they may be
  truly free,
  So that their lives might count in your struggle.

As for us, may we live in memory of the saints who have
gone before us.
May we live this day in honor of _____.
All this we pray—
  In the name of Yahweh,
    The martyrs of Christ's revolution,
      The new heaven and the new earth,

As it was promised in the beginning,
  Must be now,
And will be forever.
Amen.

Sext [Noonday]

O Restless One, come to my assistance.
O Gentle One, make haste to help us.

For the gift of this midday rest, I give you thanks.
Yahweh, the day is partly over, and partly yet to be.
In your presence,
    Help me pause . . .
        Let go . . .
            Feel again . . .
                Be fully here — now.

In quietness and in trust shall be our strength.
I am in the world, and sometimes this morning
    I was with it,
    And sometimes I was not,
    And sometimes I couldn't tell the difference.
Where is the vision we saw together?
Abba, help me with priorities and perspectives.
    Amma, help me re-remember when . . .
        And how . . .
           And *why* . . .
              Or if at all.

Accept the works I have done thus far.
    Blow your breath on what I have "blown."
        Help them come to completion.
    Forgive me when I blunted the new struggling to be
    born,
And when I settled for just getting it done.

Touch those whom with carelessness I have hurt.
    Forgive where I have not heard well—
        Where I have not seen behind the eyes and
        beneath the words,
            Where I took things personally,
        Where I kept moving myself into the center
            Of what was going on.

Thank you for letting me begin again.
Give me the discernment to participate in your yearnings
and dreams.
Let me revel in your faithfulness,
    Trusting in all things:
        Your kind leading,
            Your gentle ferociousness,
                Your restless peace—
For me, and for every sparrow.

This is the day, my God, that you have given—and
re-given.
    Help me rejoice and be glad.
        I return now to the tasks before me.
            May I live as good news to the poor
                As release to the captives,

As recovery of sight to the blind,
As liberty to the oppressed,
And as promise of the Year of Jubilee
For us all.

All this we pray—
In the name of Yahweh,
The martyrs of Christ's revolution,
The new heaven and the new earth,
As it was promised in the beginning,
Must be now,
And will be forever.
Amen.

Vespers [Sundown]

O God, come to our assistance.
O Liberator, make haste to help me.

You are the God
Of Abraham and Sarah,
Rebecca and Isaac,
Of Jacob and Rachel,
Of Zipporah and Moses,
Ruth and Naomi,
David and Jonathan,
Mary and Joseph,
Mary Magdalene and Jesus.

Therefore my soul magnifies you and my spirit rejoices in you,
    O God our Savior—
Because you have regarded the lowly people—
    Because you, the Almighty One, have done great things—
    Because you are scattering the proud in the imagina-
    tions of their hearts,
    And are pulling down the mighty from their thrones,
    And are exalting the lowly.
The hungry, O God, you will fill with good things,
    And the rich you will send empty away.

O God, help us to believe in the impossible—
    For with you all things are possible.
May we as Christians embrace as sisters and brothers
    All whose color and origin and gender compose our
    human rainbow.
Help us to glory in your declaration that in Christ there is
    Neither Jew nor Greek,
        Slave nor free,
            Male nor female—
                Nor "homosexuals,"
            Nor "witches,"
        Nor "communists,"
    Nor any other victims of our "inquisitions"—
For in Christ we are all one.

When reviled, may we bless.
    When persecuted, may we endure.
        When slandered, may we conciliate.
In willingness to be regarded as refuse of the world,
    And the offscouring of all,
        May we follow our crucified Brother.

Teach us about the extra shoes in our closet,
    Our clothing in abundance,
        Our savings in excess,
    Our homes more than needed—
That, in truth, they belong to the naked, the penniless,
and the homeless.

May we live for the Holy City
    Where on the twelve gates of Hiroshima are the
    words "Never Again."
        Where the ghettos shine like precious stones;
        Where the reservations bloom as after a spring rain;
        And where the victims of battering begin and end
        their days without fear.
Lord, we believe; help thou our unbelief.

Unto you, O God, we offer
    The works of our hands,
    The ideas of our minds,
    The feelings of our bodies,
    And the dreams and visions of our hearts.
We offer them to You:
    As the *Refining One*, make beauty of them.
    As the *Incarnate One*, take them into yourself.
    As the *Driving Spirit*, carry on without us this night.
At this close of the day, gift us with the refreshment of
knowing
    That this day we have been co-creators with you.

May the souls of the faithful, and unfaithful, departed—
    Through the mercy of God,
        Rest in peace.

Eternal rest grant unto them, O Christ,
    And let perpetual light shine upon them,
        That they may find themselves at home at last with
        You.

All this we pray—
    In the name of Yahweh,
        The martyrs of Christ's revolution,
            The new heaven and the new earth,
        As it was promised in the beginning,
    Must be now,
And will be forever.
Amen.

Compline [Bedtime]

O Yahweh,
If we live, we live to you.
And if we die, we die to you.
So whether we live or whether we die,
We are yours!

You are in our midst, *O Creator;* your image we bear.
Do not forsake us, Abba our God.
Into your hands, Lord, I commend my spirit.
May you so surround us with your acceptance
That we may have a restful night
    And a peaceful death.

You are in our midst, *O Christ*; your name we bear.
Do not forsake us, Emmanuel our God.
Into your hands, Lord, I commend my spirit.
May you so shelter us in the shadow of your wings
That we may have a restful night
> And a peaceful death.

You are in our midst, *O Spirit*; your restlessness we bear.
Do not forsake us, Alpha our God.
Into your hands, Omega, I commend my spirit.
May you so wrap us in the mantle of your Love
That we may have a restful night
> And a peaceful death.

Take, Lord, receive—
> All my liberty, my memory, my understanding, my entire will.
>> Give me only your love and your grace;
>> That is enough for me.

Take, Lord, receive—
> All I have and possess, you have given to me. Now I return it.
>> Give me only your love and your grace;
>> That is enough for me.

Take, Lord, receive—
> All is yours now. Dispose of it wholly according to your yearnings.
>> Give me only your love and your grace;
>> That is enough for me.

Let not the darkness descend
> On the hurts I have inflicted this day.

The good I would do is not always what I have
done,
And the harm from which I pledged to refrain, is
what I have done.
God, forgive me, that tomorrow I may make amends as I can.

Let not the darkness descend on the hurts that have been
inflicted on me this day.
May I not take them personally,
But hold the belief that "they knew not what they
were doing."
God, forgive them, and me,
That tomorrow I may heal what I can in these relationships.

And now,
At this time of sleep, as at the moment of my death,
May we rest with you, O Christ, in God.
Still me with the revelation that it is you,
Not I,
Who are God.

May, then, it be in tranquillity that I relinquish now my
hold on life,
That in joy I may let the world turn without me
tonight.
Fill this night with your radiance,
As into your hands, O Lord, I commend my spirit.

Protect us, Lord, as we stay awake.
Watch over us as we sleep,
That awake,
We may keep watch with Christ,

And asleep,
    We may rest in your peace.

All this we pray—
    In the name of Yahweh,
        The martyrs of Christ's revolution,
            The new heaven and the new earth,
      As it was promised in the beginning,
    Must be now,
And will be forever.
Amen.

Two-Week Schedule
for Daily Use of Psalms

An arrangement of the 150 psalms so that they correspond with the daily rhythms of the Offices, using all the psalms in a two-week period.

First Week Psalms

Vigils
(Yearning)

SUNDAY	MONDAY	TUESDAY	WEDNESDAY	THURSDAY	FRIDAY	SATURDAY
46	53	3	38	5	22	13
51	59	17	55:1-15	7	22	56
62	60	54	55:16-24	14	88	71
102:1-12	109: 1-19	86	94	61	44:1-7	73
102:13-26	109: 20-31	107	9:1-21	143	44: 18-27	74
150	116:1-9	27	9:22-	116: 10-19, 117	34	26

Lauds
(Praise)

SUNDAY	MONDAY	TUESDAY	WEDNESDAY	THURSDAY	FRIDAY	SATURDAY
8	65	19	57	132	89:1-19	139:1-14
47	144	146	87	67	89:20-53	139:15-24
148	112	24	96	147:1-11	20	98

Sext
(Mission)

SUNDAY	MONDAY	TUESDAY	WEDNESDAY	THURSDAY	FRIDAY	SATURDAY
119: (1-32)	119: (33–56)	119: (57–80)	119: (81–104)	119: (105–128)	119: (129–152)	119: (153–176)

Vespers
(Thanksgiving)

SUNDAY	MONDAY	TUESDAY	WEDNESDAY	THURSDAY	FRIDAY	SATURDAY
75	81	103	127	33:1–11	18:1–16	106:1–31
105:1–25	93	141	136	33:12–22	18:17-33	106:32–48
105:26–45	121	118	145	99	18:34–51	111

Compline
(Closure)

SUNDAY	MONDAY	TUESDAY	WEDNESDAY	THURSDAY	FRIDAY	SATURDAY
4	4	4	4	4	4	4
91	91	91	91	91	91	91

Second Week Psalms

Vigils
(Yearning)

SUNDAY	MONDAY	TUESDAY	WEDNESDAY	THURSDAY	FRIDAY	SATURDAY
36	68:1–19	12	6	35:1–16	49	63
39	68:20-36	25	64	35:17–28	31:1–19	80
43	70	28	142	41	31:20–25	101
120	95	40:1–8	78:1–8	79	69:1–13	123
140	129	40:9–18	78:9–39	83	69:14–37	137
90	130	42	78:40–72	48	77	20

Lauds
(Praise)

SUNDAY	MONDAY	TUESDAY	WEDNESDAY	THURSDAY	FRIDAY	SATURDAY
104:1–23	112	24	96	147:1–11	29	66
104:24–35	113	98	97	147:12–20	100	149
134	87	132	85	33	47	148

Sext
(Mission)

SUNDAY	MONDAY	TUESDAY	WEDNESDAY	THURSDAY	FRIDAY	SATURDAY
107:1–22	21	2	37:1–24	73	50	58
107:23–43	15	82	37:25–40	110	52	76

Vespers
(Thanksgiving)

SUNDAY	MONDAY	TUESDAY	WEDNESDAY	THURSDAY	FRIDAY	SATURDAY
114	1	84	23	11	16	125
115	45	91	32	85	122	126
124	30	131	134	138	133	128

Compline
(Closure)

SUNDAY	MONDAY	TUESDAY	WEDNESDAY	THURSDAY	FRIDAY	SATURDAY
4	4	4	4	4	4	4
91	91	91	91	91	91	91

Sentence Completion Exercise

Useful for recollection and in spiritual
direction for seeing one's time as a
pilgrimage. Write the first thing that
comes to mind.

1. I like
2. The happiest time is
3. I want to know
4. Back home
5. I regret
6. The best
7. What annoys me most is
8. Other people
9. A mother
10. I feel
11. My greatest fear is
12. In school
13. I can't
14. As a child
15. My nerves
16. I suffer
17. I failed
18. Much of the time
19. The future
20. I need
21. I am best when

22. I hate
23. The only trouble
24. I wish
25. Secretly I
26. My greatest worry is
27. My greatest longing is
28. I can't understand what makes me
29. My worst
30. I envy
31. My looks
32 . I feel most proud when
33. I am sorry that
34. I get pleasure by
35. I am ashamed because
36. If I had
37. What makes me angry is
38. The difference between mother and dad was
39. I hope
40. I most feel like smashing something when
41. If I had my way
42. I measure personal success by
43. When work piles up
44. The weakest part of me is
45. The most important thing in life is

Image Association Inventory

This tool is useful for discerning one's autobiography
as a pilgrimage. Individuals may use it themselves,
but it is particularly useful with a spiritual director or
in group discernment.

Instructions: This assessment works best when someone reads the
list of questions in fairly rapid fashion, forcing the person(s) to respond
without time to think through what one "ought" to say.

1. Who are you? (Ask and respond three times.)
2. Who told you who you are? (Ask and respond three times.)
3. Who tells you now who you are? (Ask and respond three times.)
4. Name the five most important things you do in a typical day.
5. Name the five most important things that have happened to you in the recent past.
6. Who are your five most important persons?
7. What three things are you willing to die for?
8. What one thing are you willing to live for?
9. What one thing would you most want to take . . .
   on a one-month vacation?
   to jail?
   where you are going this weekend?
10. I am most myself when I am where?
11. I am most myself when I wear what?
11. I am most myself when I travel how?
12. I am most myself when I am with whom?
13. Place after each of the following a number between

10 (high importance) and 1 (unimportant):

A. House
B. Spouse
C. Work
D. The local church
E. Success
F. Faithfulness
G. Recognition
H. Security
I. Children
J. Car
K. God
L. People
M. Myself
N. Afterlife
O. Money
P. Travel
Q. Helping
R. Leisure
S. Being first
T. Life

14. Place after each of the following words the first word that comes to mind:

A. Jesus
B. Fear
C. Kingdom
D. Worship
E. Dream
F. Fun
G. Food
H. Church
I. Sex
J. Death

15. What three wounds do you most resent having to suffer?
16. What gifts are you most grateful for?
17. Who are your three most important heroes or heroines?
18. Name three of the most crucial decisions for which you were most responsible.
19. Name three of the most crucial decisions for which you were not responsible.
20. What three persons have you hurt the most?
21. What three persons have hurt you the most?
22. What three persons have you loved the most?
23. What three persons have loved you the most?
24. Identify your three most lasting guilts.
25. Name the three things you like most about yourself.
26. What three things do you most dislike about yourself?
27. Name the three reasons why you do most of the things you do.
28. What would you want, if you could have anything you wanted?
29. What would you do, if you could do anything you wanted?
30. Where would you go, if you could go anywhere you wanted?
31. What would you be, if you could be anything you wanted?
32. With whom would you choose to be, if you could be with anyone you wanted?
33. What would you want to have said about you at your funeral?
34. What period of your life would be most distressing to have to live again? Why?
35. What period of your life would you most like to relive? Why?

Prayers to Honor
Each Other's Stories

Prayers for discernment groups seeking spiritual growth
by sharing personal stories. These are very important
for establishing committed confidentiality.

These two prayers were composed by a woman who was
terrified by the thought that someone in the group with
which she would share her story would desecrate it by
violating confidentiality. By praying these prayers in
unison, she and others were enabled to trust and share
honestly their fragile autobiographies.

Prayer for Openness

Author of all our stories, who imagined us into being, be
    with us as we share the plots of our lives.
Create a sacred space where the words we speak will be
    heard with compassion, not judgment.
Remind us to reveal only as much of the mystery of who
    we are as we feel comfortable disclosing.
Help us to read between the lines of each other's lives
    and see the themes that connect each scene together.
Keep us from the temptation to tell each other's stories,
    or to use anything that is said today against one another.
Thank you for the opportunity to know who you are as
    we discover your incarnation in each other.
Amen.

Prayer for Closure

Creator of us all, we see you in each other's eyes,
    hear you in each other's words,
        learn who you are as we learn to understand
        ourselves.
Help us to leave this space feeling whole, not broken;
    healed, not wounded;
        loved, not despised.
We have experienced the sacrament of sharing our stories,
    and promise to keep them sacred.
Amen.

Endnotes

Chapter Two—Birth as a Religious Event: Beginning the Spritual Journey

1. William Kraft, *Psychology of Nothingness* (Philadelphia: Westminster, 1974), 104.
2. T.S. Eliot, "East Coker," in *Four Quartets,* in *The Complete Poems and Plays* (New York: Harcourt, Brace, & Co., 1934), 126-7.
3. Simon Weil, *Waiting for God* (New York: Harper, 1973), 210.
4. *Handbook for Today's Catholic* (Liguiori, Mo.: Liguori Publications, 1994), 46.
5. Matthew Kelty, *Aspects of the Monastic Calling* (Gethsemane Monastery, Trappist, Ky., n.d.), 11.
6. T.S. Eliot, "Burned Norton," *Four Quartets* (NY: Harcourt, Brace & Co., 1952). p. 119; Ibid, "Little Gidding." p. 144.
7. Andre Louf, *Tuning In to Grace* (Kalamazoo, Mich.: Cistercian Publications, 1992), 76.
8. Sigmund Freud, *Civilization and Its Discontents* (New York: W. W. Norton, 1961), 11-15.
9. Charles Wesley, From the hymn "Love Divine, All Loves Excelling," *The United Methodist Hymnal* (Nashville: The United Methodist Publishing House, 1989), #384.

10. Edwin Hatch, "Breathe on Me, Breath of God," Ibid., #420.

Chapter Three—Time and Space as Relationship

1. H.R. Niebuhr, *Faith and Ethics* (New York: Harper & Brothers, 1957), 42.
2. H.R. Neibuhr, *The Meaning of Revelation* (NY: MacMillan, 1946), pp. 59ff.
3. Ibid., pp. 37–38.
4. Ibid., p. 40.
6. Ibid., p. 60.
7. St. Benedict, *Rule for Monasteries* (Collegeville, Minn., 1935), 2.

Chapter Four—Theologically Based Experience

1. Henry D. Thoreau, *Walden* (Princeton: Princeton University Press, 1989), p. 90
2. See W. Paul Jones, *Theological Worlds: Understanding the Alternative Rhythms of Christian Belief* (Nashville: Abingdon Press, 1989). W. Paul Jones, *Worlds Within a Congregation: Dealing with Theological Diversity* (Nashville: Abingdon Press, 2000).
3. The following is the result of a dialogue with Fr. Kelty, OCSO.

Chapter Five—Expansive Time

1. Although the office of Prime is no longer observed, the idea remains the same.
2. Fr. Alkiviades Calivas, "Introduction," *The Divine Liturgy of Saint John Chrysostom* (Medfield, Mass.: Olive Tree Press, 1988).
3. Fyodar Dostoyevsky, *The Brothers Karamazov* (NY: The Modern Library, 1950), p. xviii.
4. Bernhard W. Anderson, *The Unfolding Drama of the Bible* (NY: Association Press, 1953), pp.12f.
5. See Jones, *Theological Worlds.*
6. Jones, *Theological Worlds,* and Jones, *Worlds Within a Congregation.*
7. James Fowler and Sam Keen, *Life Maps* (Waco, Tex.: Word Books, 1978), 123.
8. Audrey LaPorte Vest, *Why Celebrate Jubilee?* (Liguori, Mo.: Liguori Publications, 1999).

Chapter Six—Time as Lived

1. Gertrude the Great of Helfa, *Spiritual Exercises* (Kalamazoo, Mich.: Cistercian Publications, 1989), 112.
2. Ibid., p.22.
3. *The Order of Prayer in the Liturgy of the Hours and the Celebration of the Eucharist,* (Mahwah, N.J.: Paulist Press, 1999), 18.
4. *The Liturgy of the Hours* Vigils for July 23 , Vol. 3 (New York: Catholic Book Publishing Co., 1970), 1550.
5. *The Order of Prayer,* 94.

6. Thomas Oden, *The Community of Celebration* (Nashville: The National Methodist Student Movement, 1964), 107.
7. *Bernard of Clairvaux: Selected Works* (New York: Paulist Press, 1987), 199.
8. See Tilden Edward's list of contrasts between Sabbath and Ministry. *Sabbath Time* (Minneapolis: Seabury Press, 1982), 41-42.
9. In what follows, I have used some of the images contained in the "Introduction" to the no longer used *Latin Breviary* (Collegeville: The Liturgical Press, 1964).
10. T.S. Eliot, Choruses, from "The Rock."
11. T.S. Eliot, "The Dry Salvages," in *Four Quartets.*
12. Thornton Wilder, *Our Town* (New York: Harper and Row, 1957), 99. Douglas Burton-Christie called my attention to the theme of "attentiveness" in Wilder. "Christ in Ten Thousand Places: Cultivating the Art of Attention," *Cistercian Studies* 35 (No. 1), 113-123.
13. Ibid., 120.

Chapter Seven—The Triduum

1. T.S. Eliot, *Murder in the Cathedral,* in *The Complete Poems and Plays* (New York: Harcourt, Brace, and Co., 1952), 208.

Chapter Eight—Conclusion

1. Luke 1:78—Translation, International Consultation on English Texts, *The Liturgy of the Hours* (New York: Catholic Book Publishing Co, 1975)
2. Matthew Kelty, *Sermons in a Monastery* (Kalamazoo, MI: Cistercian Publications, Inc., 1983), pp.46–47.